D0792386

The History of J. F. Shea Co.

The History of J. F. Shea Co.

Jeffrey L. Rodengen

Richard F. Hubbard

Edited by Melody Maysonet
Design and layout by Rachelle Donley

Write Stuff Enterprises, Inc.
1001 South Andrews Avenue
Second Floor
Fort Lauderdale, FL 33316
1-800-900-Book (1-800-900-2665)
(954) 462-6657
www.writestuffbooks.com

Copyright © 2004 by Write Stuff Enterprises, Inc. All rights reserved. No part of this book may be reproduced or transmitted in any form by any means, electronic or mechanical, including photocopying and recording, or by any information storage or retrieval system, without permission in writing from the publisher.

Publisher's Cataloging in Publication

Rodengen, Jeffrey L.
    The History of J. F. Shea Co. / Jeffrey L. Rodengen and Richard F. Hubbard ; edited by Melody Maysonet; design and layout by Rachelle Donley. — 1st ed.
    p. cm.
    Includes bibliographical references and index.
    LCCN 2002115060
    ISBN 0-945903-91-X

    1. J.F. Shea Co.—History. 2. Construction industry—United States—History. I. Hubbard, Richard F. II. Title

HD9715.U54J37 2003   338.7'624'0973
                                              QBI03-200920

Library of Congress
Catalog Card Number 2002115060

ISBN 0-945903-91-X

Completely produced in the
United States of America
10 9 8 7 6 5 4 3 2 1

Also by Jeffrey L. Rodengen

The Legend of Chris-Craft

IRON FIST:
The Lives of Carl Kiekhaefer

Evinrude-Johnson and
The Legend of OMC

Serving the Silent Service:
The Legend of Electric Boat

The Legend of
Dr Pepper/Seven-Up

The Legend of Honeywell

The Legend of Briggs & Stratton

The Legend of Ingersoll-Rand

The Legend of Stanley:
150 Years of The Stanley Works

The MicroAge Way

The Legend of Halliburton

The Legend of York International

The Legend of Nucor Corporation

The Legend of Goodyear:
The First 100 Years

The Legend of AMP

The Legend of Cessna

The Legend of VF Corporation

The Spirit of AMD

The Legend of Rowan

New Horizons:
The Story of Ashland Inc.

The History of American Standard

The Legend of Mercury Marine

The Legend of Federal-Mogul

Against the Odds:
Inter-Tel—The First 30 Years

The Legend of Pfizer

State of the Heart:
The Practical Guide to Your Heart
and Heart Surgery
with Larry W. Stephenson, M.D.

The Legend of
Worthington Industries

The Legend of IBP, Inc.

The Legend of
Trinity Industries, Inc.

The Legend of
Cornelius Vanderbilt Whitney

The Legend of Amdahl

The Legend of Litton Industries

The Legend of Gulfstream

The Legend of Bertram
with David A. Patten

The Legend of
Ritchie Bros. Auctioneers

The Legend of ALLTEL
with David A. Patten

The Yes, you can of
Invacare Corporation
with Anthony L. Wall

The Ship in the Balloon:
The Story of Boston Scientific
and the Development of
Less-Invasive Medicine

The Legend of
Day & Zimmermann

The Legend of Noble Drilling

Fifty Years of Innovation:
Kulicke & Soffa

Biomet—From Warsaw
to the World
with Richard F. Hubbard

NRA: An American Legend

The Heritage and Values
of RPM, Inc.

The Marmon Group:
The First Fifty Years

The Legend of Grainger

The Legend of
The Titan Corporation
with Richard F. Hubbard

The Legend of Discount Tire Co.
with Richard F. Hubbard

The Legend of Polaris
with Richard F. Hubbard

The Legend of La-Z-Boy
with Richard F. Hubbard

The Legend of McCarthy
with Richard F. Hubbard

InterVoice:
Twenty Years of Innovation
with Richard F. Hubbard

Jefferson-Pilot Financial:
A Century of Excellence
with Richard F. Hubbard

The Legend of HCA
with Richard F. Hubbard

The Legend of Werner Enterprises
with Richard F. Hubbard

TABLE OF CONTENTS

INTRODUCTION

CHARLIE SHEA'S worn, floppy hat is symbolic of the J. F. Shea Co., Inc. Since the company's founding, the Sheas have been more than managers and owners. Dust-covered, wearing worn boots, with calloused hands and sweaty faces, they have sometimes been mistaken for hired hands. They were reared in the family business, and they know from experience the meaning of hard work. On top of that, few builders can boast of having been involved in three of the 20th century's top 10 construction achievements (the interstate highway system, the Golden Gate Bridge, and Hoover Dam), and fewer still can list those achievements as only a small part of their heritage. The J. F. Shea Co., Inc., is among these.

The company's rich history took root in 1846 when Austin Shea immigrated to the United States from Ireland. He and his wife settled in Ohio and had a son, John Francis Shea, whose ambition led him to start a plumbing business in Portland, Oregon. When John Francis opened the J. F. Shea Plumbing Company in 1881, he couldn't have known his enterprise would endure two world wars and numerous economic recessions to thrive in the 21st century.

As Portland expanded in the late 19th century, Shea built much of the city's infrastructure. Three of John's nine children—Charlie, Gilbert, and Edmund—learned the basics of infrastructure construction at an early age. As John grew older, Charlie took over the family business, and soon Shea was taking on major underground piping and tunnel work.

During World War I, Shea installed plumbing and heating facilities in ships and by the early 1920s had become a major sewer contractor. Thanks to Charlie's assertive style and reputation for hard work, Shea was able to win large contracts such as the sewer system of the Portland Seawall and an enormous water pipeline in California dubbed "the biggest experiment in the history of pipe laying."

After their father died in 1926, Charlie, Gil, and Ed went on to build major tunnels in Oregon. Meanwhile, the Sheas were earning a reputation as exceptional employers, for they provided professional supervision as well as excellent wages.

During the Great Depression, Shea helped build some of the country's most challenging construction projects: The colossal Hoover Dam involved excavating 6 million cubic yards of rock and dirt and pouring 4.3 million cubic yards of concrete. Golden Gate Bridge was the longest suspension bridge in the world. And the San Francisco–Oakland Bay Bridge is the longest steel high-level bridge in the world. In the years leading up to World War II, Shea helped build such immense structures as Bonneville Dam on the Columbia River and the difficult Parker Dam, which was the deepest dam in the world.

After Charlie died in 1942, Gil became president of the company and led it through the difficult World War II years when labor and materials were scarce. During this time, Shea showed its characteristic resiliency and began investing in "smokestack" ventures. It even built Liberty ships for the British.

In the late 1950s and early 1960s, John (son of Gil) and Edmund and Peter (sons of Edmund) reestablished Shea as a major contender in heavy construction. Among other achievements, Shea built many tunnel and pipeline projects that were vital to the California Aqueduct, a "man-made river" that provided water, flood control, and hydroelectric power. Shea was instrumental in building the nation's interstate highway system and was heavily involved in building the Bay Area Rapid Transit (BART) system, which links Oakland and the East San Francisco Bay area with San Francisco.

Shea had been successful enough in heavy construction that it could afford to broaden its scope during the recessionary economy of the 1970s when heavy construction work tapered off. Realizing the future belonged to computer chip, semiconductor, software, and biotech companies, Shea began investing much of its heavy-construction income in start-up companies.

The company also diversified into homebuilding and property management with Shea Homes and Shea Properties. The homebuilding industry hit a slump in the early 1980s, thanks to high interest rates and soaring inflation. At the same time, the heavy-construction market was very slow. Being a private company that did not have to answer to shareholders, Shea shrank itself and was able to persevere. By the time the heavy-construction market recovered in the late 1980s, Shea was positioned to bid successfully on a variety of projects.

By then, Shea Homes had emerged as a more significant player in the homebuilding business, thanks in large part to its evolution from a single-family homebuilder into a developer of master-planned communities. Shea Properties, meanwhile, had evolved into a multifaceted company.

Like other builders, Shea sustained significant losses in the real estate depression of the early 1990s. Excessively high debt crippled many homebuilders in California—but not Shea. Shea Homes was able to weather the recessionary storm better than most other builders because it had diversified into other markets and because it was privately held. Both Shea Homes and Shea Properties embarked on a wave of growth in the late 1990s and into the next century. In the meantime, Shea was working on a variety of important heavy-construction projects.

Shea has endured some difficult times during its long history, but today the company is more diverse and more widely respected than ever. Shea's culture is built on a foundation of respect for the customer and fellow employees, and it chooses contractors not only by the lowest bidder but by the quality and safety of their work. John, Edmund, and Peter Shea are among the industry's finest businessmen and most respected managers, and the next generation of Sheas—which includes Peter Shea, Jr. and John Morrissey—are well on their way to continuing the traditions of quality and caring that John Francis Shea began in 1881.

ACKNOWLEDGMENTS

MANY PEOPLE ASSISTED IN THE research, preparation, and publication of *The History of J. F. Shea Co.*

This book would not have been possible without the professional skills of our talented research assistant, Bob Wisehart. Bob's writing and research talents went a long way toward making this book a success. Senior Editor Melody Maysonet oversaw the text and photos. Graphic design by Rachelle Donley brought the story to vivid life.

Several key people associated with Shea lent their invaluable efforts to the book's completion, sharing their experience, providing valuable oversight for accuracy, and helping guide the book's development from outline to final form: John Shea, president of the J. F. Shea Co., Inc.; Edmund Shea, executive vice president; Peter Shea, executive vice president; Jim Shontere, chief financial officer; and Sally Chieppor, executive assistant to John Shea and Jim Shontere.

Many other Shea executives, employees, retirees, family members, and friends greatly enriched the book by discussing their experiences. The authors extend particular gratitude to these men and women for their candid recollections and guidance: Buck Atherton, Robert Bridges, Jeff Dritley, Bob Gordon, Roy Humphreys, Norm Hutchins, Max Johnson, Alison Shea Knoll, Merv Koster, Ron Lakey, Jim Marquardt, Allen Myers, Bill Morris, Dorothy Murphy, Eugene Murphy, Robb Pigg, Pete Seley, Edmund Shea III, Gilbert Shea III, Jim Shea, John Shea, Jr., Peter Shea, Jr., Mary Ellen Simon, Les Thomas, Carrie Shea Tilton, and Bruce Varker.

Special thanks are extended to the dedicated staff and associates at Write Stuff Enterprises, Inc.: Jon VanZile, former executive editor; Heather Deeley, associate editor; Torey Marcus, executive editor; Debra Kronowitz, senior editor; Peter Donald, senior editor; Bonnie Freeman and Kevin Allen, copy editors; Sandy Cruz, senior art director; Dennis Shockley, art director; Mary Aaron, transcriptionist; Barbara Koch, indexer; Bruce Borich, production manager; Marianne Roberts, vice president of administration; Sherry Hasso, bookkeeper; Julie Castro, executive assistant to Jeffrey L. Rodengen; and Lars Jessen, director of worldwide marketing.

In 1881, John Francis Shea (seated center) founded the J. F. Shea Plumbing Company, the predecessor of the J. F. Shea Co., Inc. Standing, from left: Anne, Charles, Ivelou, and Gilbert. Seated, from left: Frank, Edmund, Mrs. Anna McGinn Shea, Dorothy, John F. Shea, Mabel, and Ethel.

CHAPTER ONE

PLANTING ROOTS

1846–1906

[John Francis Shea] owed his prosperity to tireless effort, good management and close conformity to a high standard of commercial ethics. . . . His many good qualities endeared him to all with whom he was associated.

—Excerpt from *History of the Columbia River Valley*

IN MANY WAYS J. F. SHEA Co., Inc., is the quintessential American success story.

An uneducated immigrant came to the United States. He eventually settled in Dayton, Ohio, found work as a laborer, married, and raised a family.

A father's ambition for a better life was passed on to his son, who realized that whatever he wanted, he wouldn't find it in Dayton. Barely out of his teens, sometime in the mid-1870s, the son followed Horace Greeley's advice to "turn your face to the great west and there build up your home and fortune."[1]

After working for a year in San Francisco, the younger Shea settled in Portland, Oregon,[2] where he started his own plumbing company in 1881.[3] Through his hard work and integrity, the company grew to become one of the most successful of its kind in the Pacific Northwest. His son eventually took over the business, which expanded, grew, and changed as the country expanded, grew, and changed. Each succeeding generation inherited the business.

From that start as a modest, one-man plumbing company in Portland more than 120 years ago, J. F. Shea Co., Inc., has evolved into a thriving, diverse, multibillion-dollar corporation that ranks as one of the nation's oldest and largest privately held companies and as one of the nation's leading homebuilders.

The name Shea is as rich in achievement as it is in history. According to a poll of the editors of heavy-construction trade journals, Shea participated in three of the 20th century's top 10 construction achievements: the Golden Gate Bridge, Hoover Dam, and the interstate highway system.[4]

The story of J. F. Shea Co., Inc., is as remarkable as it is unique, truly an American success story.

The Beginning

In 1846, 28-year-old Austin Shea emigrated with his family from Ireland to America.[5] He was one of thousands of Irish fleeing the dreadful potato famine that killed one out of every nine people in Ireland, more than 1 million people

---

John F. Shea was a self-made man. His prosperous plumbing company in Portland, Oregon, initially manufactured, sold, and serviced plumbing fixtures and beer refrigeration systems.

altogether, in the 1840s and early 1850s.[6] Though the ship the Shea family sailed on was named *Speed,* the passage across the stormy North Atlantic was typically slow and difficult, especially for steerage passengers, who lived belowdecks deep in the bowels of the ship. Then when the Sheas disembarked in their new country, they were detained an extra day at the wharfs of Manhattan, New York, the main point of entry for immigrants on the East Coast, because they arrived on Independence Day, a national holiday.[7]

Like many others before him, Austin Shea apparently decided that the teeming tenements of New York City were not the place to make his fortune. In time he moved to the Midwest.

Austin Shea, father of John F. Shea, was an Irishman who immigrated with his family to the United States. They landed at the wharfs of Manhattan, New York, in 1846.

According to *History of the Columbia River Valley,* Austin met his wife, Catherine Raidy (or Ready) Shea, in Dayton, Ohio,[8] where he found what work he could as a laborer.[9]

"Our great-grandfather worked as a day laborer," said J. F. Shea President John Shea in 1999. "He was uneducated and could neither read nor write." He even signed his will with an *X.*[10]

A son, John Francis Shea, was born in Dayton on March 14, 1855.[11] As a youngster, he was eager to improve himself and supplemented his public schooling with courses at the University of Dayton.[12] Like thousands of other young men who wanted something more out of life, Shea made the momentous decision to go west sometime in the mid-1870s.

The journey was no small undertaking. It was a time when the West was at its wildest. The James-Younger Gang was robbing banks and trains throughout Kansas and Missouri. James Butler "Wild Bill" Hickok was shot and

In 1891 John Shea moved the J. F. Shea Plumbing headquarters to this building (center of photograph), which he built at Second and Ankeny Streets in Portland, Oregon.

killed in Deadwood, South Dakota, in 1876. That same year, Lieutenant Colonel George Armstrong Custer was killed near the Little Big Horn River in what is now Montana. Shea's arduous cross-country trip took months and was a bold roll of the dice even for an ambitious young man.

When he finally reached booming San Francisco, John Shea went to work for the Donnerberg Plumbing Company, where he stayed for about a year. He was apparently highly regarded and rose rapidly in the company, eventually becoming manager.[13]

But the young man wanted to go into business for himself and decided that Portland, Oregon, was the place to do it. Shea moved north sometime in the late 1870s and in 1881 opened a plumbing shop at the corner of Sixth and Washington Streets in Portland. It would be the home of the J. F. Shea Plumbing Company for the next 10 years.[14] When the business outgrew that location, he built his own ample building at the corner of Second and Ankeny Streets. This would be the offices of J. F. Shea Plumbing for more than 30 years.[15]

The J. F. Shea Plumbing Company achieved its initial success in manufacturing, selling, and servicing plumbing fixtures and beer refrigeration systems,[16] dealing in both wholesale and retail.[17] Decades later one of John Shea's grandsons, J. F. Shea Vice President Edmund Shea,

would stay in the old wing of the Benson Hotel in Portland as a boy. He was pleased to see "J. F. Shea" engraved on the plumbing fixtures.[18]

On August 26, 1880, John Francis Shea married Anna Maria McGinn, a 20-year-old Portland native.[19] Her father, Charles McGinn, was a baker who owned his own company. A prominent and well-to-do man in the growing town, McGinn was described in *History of the Columbia River Valley* as "one of the pioneer business men of Portland."[20]

John Shea had become a pillar of his community at a relatively young age. Politically he was a staunch Republican. He was also a devout member of the Roman Catholic Church and a member of the Benevolent Order of the Elks.[21]

As busy as John Shea was with his business and a growing family, apparently his family back in Ohio was never far from his mind. For example, an 1891 letter from his sister Katie thanked him for a substantial gift, a $20 gold piece, the equivalent of several hundred dollars today.

"You will undoubtedly think I have taken my time in thanking you, but I can not express my thanks for the twenty dollar gold piece which you sent to me. . . . It was so unexpected that it was received with great joy," she wrote.[22]

In her chatty letter from Dayton, Katie updated her brother about the activities of the rest of the family and urged him to make the trip east so that the family could meet his wife and children.

"If you do not bring the children our hopes will be blighted, as Mother is really more anxious to see the children than she is to see yourself, but we are all very anxious to see Anna," she wrote.[23]

A Growing Family

John and Anna Shea had nine children: Charles, Anne, Ivelou, Frank, Mabel, Ethel, Gilbert, Edmund, and Dorothy. Such a family needed a large home, and Shea bought a two-and-a-half-story neocolonial residence at 1809 Johnson Street in Portland. Originally built for Portland lumber magnate Winslow B. Ayer, it was one of the city's showplace residences, with oak woodwork, parquet floors, several brick

Above right: Though John Shea was reserved, he was a leader in the Portland community.

Below: The Shea family house on Johnson Street in Portland has been designated a historical monument by the National Register of Historic Places. Nearly 100 years after the Sheas resided there, the house was converted into an office building occupied by attorneys.

fireplaces, and a large central staircase.[24] Given that his business was plumbing and he had such a large family, it's no surprise that Shea "added bathrooms all over the house," which was so big that it would be converted to a dozen offices almost 100 years later.[25] The home was listed on the National Register of Historic Places in 1982.[26]

Charles Austin Shea, the oldest child of John and Anna Shea, was born on November 26, 1883. By the time he was 14, Charlie was working for his father's company as a plumber's helper.[27] By the time he was 16, he was an accomplished plumber who genuinely enjoyed working with his hands and rubbing shoulders with other workers, pleasures that turned into a lifelong habit despite later wealth and success.[28] His brothers Gilbert and Edmund, who later joined the family business as partners, were considerably younger, born in 1896 and 1898 respectively.[29]

John F. Shea was a resolute Irishman. In 1914 he contributed $5 to help arm and equip the Irish National Volunteers, and in 1923 he was a member of the "Lang Syne" Society.

As the years passed, with a prosperous business and a growing, happy family, John Shea acquired considerable stature in his community. He was both respected and liked.

"Diligent and successful in business, he left the deep impress of his individuality upon his work, and he belonged to that class of men who, although modest and unassuming, nevertheless shape the character and influence the development of the communities in which they live," observed one writer. "His ability and energy placed him in a position of leadership. He installed the plumbing in many of Portland's fine residences and public buildings and owed his prosperity to tireless effort, good management and close conformity to a high standard of commercial ethics. . . . His many good

qualities endeared him to all with whom he was associated."[30]

In an interview not long before her death in 1988, Dorothy Shea Murphy, the youngest of John and Anna Shea's nine children, fondly remembered life in the Shea home. "My father was a very quiet man . . . very dignified," she recalled. "He never talked over the business with mother. Business didn't interest her in the least. . . . Now the men talk over the business with their wives, but father didn't. I don't think in those days anyone did."[31]

In addition to his plumbing business, apparently he did well in real estate, too. "Father was a self-made man," Dorothy said. "He built apartment houses and a hotel in Portland. We received $3,000 a month in rentals. That was a lot of money in those days. We always lived very well." Apparently John Shea didn't rule out all business talk at home. According to his daughter, "Father said that in the construction business you live up to your contract. If you don't, you pay the penalty. That's the way he ran his company and lived his life."[32]

Dorothy also remembered another important force in the home.

Mother was a very influential person in our family. Charlie would come to Mother with his troubles and she was always level headed. No matter what the story was, she'd handle it in a very calming way. She would warn him and counsel him because my father would just say, "Oh you're just crazy," or something like that. She was a very influential person in his life and in all our lives. She made a beautiful home for all of us.[33]

A Family Business

The J. F. Shea Plumbing Company was involved in the construction of much of Portland's infrastructure during the city's extraordinary

---

The J. F. Shea Plumbing Company worked on Portland's Bull Run Water Supply System. Pictured is the Bull Run campsite. *(Photo courtesy Oregon Historical Society)*

growth spurt around the turn of the century. Shea's major contracts included several sewer and storm drain projects and substantial work on Portland's Bull Run Water Supply System, which still supplies water to the city more than 100 years later.

Whether as a result of their father's insistence or of their own choosing, Charles, Gilbert, and Edmund were involved in the most basic aspects of construction from an early age. All three worked "from the ground up."[34] In time, that would become a Shea tradition passed from one generation to the next. As Dorothy Shea Murphy said, when her father reached an age where he "didn't do the dirty work . . . Gilbert, Edmund, and Charlie did."[35]

After graduating from high school in 1902, Charlie didn't take long to establish himself as a confident and aggressive, up-and-coming young man whose drive and ambition often outstripped and sometimes worried his more conservative father.

"Charlie was involved in the company early," his sister recalled. "[He was] always much more daring than father ever was and that used to worry father a little bit. Father used to stew about Charlie getting in too deep. [Father] was much more conservative and that used to bother him. I remember when we were at the family beach house and everybody would go clamming. Charlie would get so many clams the whole back porch would be full of clams. Anything he did, he did in a big way."[36]

Like his father before him, Charlie Shea wanted to make his own way. He left Portland for Tacoma, Washington, where he started an independent career in sewer construction, working for Twohy Brothers, a construction company owned by Jim and John Twohy, who became good friends of the Sheas and would work with them several times in the years to come.

"He was doing well in Tacoma, working with the Twohy Brothers," his sister said. "Charlie was a great friend of Jim and John Twohy. They were making him their head man."[37]

But back home in Portland, his father was having trouble. It wasn't much at first, certainly nothing alarming. But it promised to get worse. It was increasingly difficult for John Shea to run the business by himself, and Gilbert and Edmund were still too young to help enough.

"Father was getting older, and he had sciatica and it was bothering him," Dorothy said. "Father had several contracts, and it was all just too much for him."[38]

And so came a critical point in the history of the Shea companies. The father needed help, and his son was the only one in the family who could provide it. According to Dorothy, "Mother wrote to Charlie and said, 'Your father needs you, and I think you should be at home and taking care of the business here.'"[39]

Despite his bright future in Tacoma, apparently Charlie Shea didn't hesitate. "He came back to Portland and got everything pulled together," his sister said. "Charlie was the man to take over. The company's early success was due to father's start and his having money at the proper moment. But Charlie was responsible for its rise. As a Portland banker once told my husband, 'There's never been anything like the rise of the J. F. Shea Co., Inc.'"[40]

Charlie Shea, firstborn son of John F. Shea, redirected his father's company to deal in underground piping and tunnel work. Though this formal portrait shows him in a suit and tie, Charlie was most often seen in worn work clothes, complete with a battered, floppy hat.

CHAPTER TWO

CARVING OUT A DESTINY

1907–1934

Few would turn down a Shea job to go elsewhere. No one treated people better than the Sheas.

—Robert L. Bridges, attorney for the J. F. Shea Co., Inc.

O N APRIL 10, 1907, five years after graduating from high school in Portland, Charlie Shea married Portland native Lessie Lind.[1] They would have four children: Maxine, Charles, Patricia, and Donald.

The next several years were a busy time for young Charlie Shea. For the first time in his life, the "pugnacious, hard-drinking little Irishman" who hated suits and ties and preferred to dress "in the style of a day laborer," including a battered, floppy hat that became his trademark, had to balance work and family.[2]

Expanding the Business

There was plenty of work, more so because the J. F. Shea Plumbing Company was changing. Despite his youth, Charlie Shea was intent on remaking his father's company. He began to transition the company's core business to underground piping and tunnel work and away from smaller contracts. He was determined to build the company into one of the best-known plumbing firms in Portland.[3]

A simple plumbing business "was too tame . . . for a free spirit like Charlie's," wrote one historian. "Once he had laid a few dozen miles of pipe in the ground, he realized that the exciting and potentially most profitable challenges of the business had usually already been faced before he ever put his pipe on the job. What he liked was clearing the right-of-way, excavating the muck and rock, shoring the trenches, driving the tunnels, and bridging the streams."[4]

By 1908 the J. F. Shea Plumbing Company had expanded into major sewer construction, with Charlie handling most of the bidding and supervising the larger jobs. Through the mid-1920s the company would build at least four major sewer and storm drain systems in Portland alone. Charlie relentlessly pushed the company to pursue bigger and more complex jobs, where the risks were as great as the rewards. By all accounts his father approved, if sometimes reluctantly. It must have been difficult for John F. Shea to ignore his more conservative instincts in favor of his son's judgment.[5]

Charlie's younger brothers Gil and Ed were coming along, too. From the time they were boys,

---

Shea used an improved excavating tool, nicknamed the "Owyhee-type mucker," on the Owyhee Irrigation Project. In 1931, the Shea Owyhee crew was able to break two world records for tunnel excavation.

it seemed clear that they were destined to join the family business. As a youngster in Portland, one of Gil's jobs was to light the lanterns in the tunnels for the night crew on local sewer jobs.[6] Unlike the impatient Charlie, who was eager to get out into the working world and do things his way, Ed and Gil both attended college. Gil, who was 12 years younger than Charlie and two years older than Ed, attended the University of California at Berkeley for two years. Ed attended Notre Dame for a year before joining the Canadian Air Force not long before the United States entered World War I. After he was discharged, Ed attended Columbia University for a year before transferring to the University of California at Berkeley, where he graduated.

"Gil and Edmund both worked in the business as boys, just like Charlie did earlier," their sister said. "They would get so dirty that Mother wouldn't allow them upstairs until they showered and changed in the basement."[7]

By 1915 it was obvious that the company needed to be reorganized to reflect Charlie's increasingly dominant role. As a result, the old company was dissolved and a new one took its place: the J. F. Shea Company. John and Charlie Shea each had a 40 percent interest. The remaining 20 percent went to 19-year-old Gil.[8] Ed Shea, then only 17, later became a partner, too.

The Sheas' unsurpassed plumbing expertise led Charlie Shea to take an unexpected detour during World War I. Charlie's old friends the Twohy brothers were the principal owners of the North Pacific Shipbuilding Company in Seattle.[9] Although the details are sketchy and the records disappeared long ago, what is certain is that the Twohys recruited Charlie for a prominent wartime position in their shipyard. Some records indicate that he was the North Pacific Shipbuilding Company's general manager from about 1917 to 1920, keeping his position with the J. F. Shea Company at the same time.[10] But according to other sources, John Twohy was the shipyard's general manager and Charlie reported to him, although it was Charlie who had hands-on management of the shipyard's production.[11]

Whatever Charlie's title might have been, it's clear that the J. F. Shea Company was responsible for installing the plumbing and heating facilities in the ships manufactured at the shipyard during this time.[12] Records indicate that the North Pacific Shipbuilding Company built 10 ships from 1917 to 1920, a reasonable production rate at a time when construction techniques were more primitive, especially considering the start-up time required to convert to a war footing.[13] The J. F. Shea Company's experience at North Pacific Shipbuilding would become invaluable when the Sheas got involved in ship-

building in a much bigger way in the years before the United States entered World War II.

By the early 1920s, the J. F. Shea Company had grown to become a major sewer contractor with a wide range of experience and a sterling reputation throughout the Pacific Northwest. Although the company had all the work it could handle, Charlie was always looking to expand and was eager to take on new challenges and seize opportunity when he could.

According to one recapitulation of the company's activity, "Following completion of the shipbuilding program early in 1920, the Sheas began construction of sewers in Seattle and Portland totaling $1,000,000. Late in 1920, Twohy [Brothers] secured a $7,000,000 contract for 300 miles of . . . concrete pavement in Maricopa County, Arizona." Although it was not directly involved in the construction, "Shea had a considerable [financial] interest" in the undertaking.[14]

In 1921, the J. F. Shea Company began a $1 million contract for field work on Portland's Bull Run water supply pipeline. This job was followed by several smaller contracts in the Pacific Northwest that totaled about $1 million. Then in 1923 and 1924, the company constructed sewers for the city of Portland under several different contracts totaling $2.5 million.[15]

These were all huge jobs at a time when a $100,000 contract was considered large, as Dorothy Shea Murphy illustrated in an anecdote about her father: "One evening the telephone rang constantly for father, and it was when he had bid on a dam . . . in Portland and got it," she said. "I think it was about $100,000. It was a lot of money then. The telephone kept ringing with people congratulating him."[16]

The mid-1920s were watershed years for the J. F. Shea Company. Shea took on two contracts that were the biggest, most public, and most difficult in the company's more than 40 years. When one of the jobs brought Shea into California in a big way, the J. F. Shea Company met its future, although no one realized it at the time.

The Portland Seawall

In 1926 the J. F. Shea Company won the contract to build the sewer system for the Portland Seawall along the Willamette River in Oregon. Shea was a subcontractor for the Pacific Bridge Company, which would build the seawall itself. Pacific Bridge and Shea would keep up a successful relationship over many years and projects.

The J. F. Shea Company received plenty of work in the 1920s. The company even had its own fleet of trucks.

The Portland Seawall was a project born of necessity. Portland badly needed to refurbish its aging waterfront and port area, which hadn't kept up with the city's growth and hadn't been improved in decades.

An article in the *Portland Oregonian* put it this way:

> *Construction of a river wall on the main west water front of Portland will be the first unit in a great work which is to contribute to the making of a new Portland. . . . The port has* simply *far outgrown the present structures along the river between Jefferson and Glisan streets, and they have become mere relics of a long past era in the city's development. . . . Discharge of sewage directly into the river served for the city's infancy but is offensive to health and to the nostrils when population has passed a third of a million and is evidently destined soon to reach half a million.*[17]

The Portland Seawall was part of an overall reconstruction of the Portland waterfront. To their dismay, property owners were asked to pay for much of the construction themselves. When several of them refused, the controversial project came under intense public scrutiny, and it took the city three years just to negotiate with the various property owners so the job could get under way.[18]

Subcontracting for the Pacific Bridge Company in 1926, the J. F. Shea Company began building the sewer system for the Portland Seawall, located on the Willamette River. *(Photo courtesy Oregon Historical Society)*

The total contract was worth $11 million, and much of the work dealt with the rising impact of automobile traffic in the area, including a scenic harbor drive along the seawall. The seawall and sewer, parts of which still exist, cost $2.7 million. The project was completed in 1929, three years after it began.[19]

The Mokelumne Pipeline

If the Portland Seawall seemed like a difficult undertaking, at least politically, what followed must have seemed almost impossible to anyone but Charlie Shea and a handful of other hard-driving visionaries.

The J. F. Shea Company had worked in California before, although not on anything as large as the project it was about to tackle. Some of the Sheas' early California contracts included subcontracting with Twohy Brothers to build an

airport at March Field, near Riverside, California,[20] and the construction of water pipelines in Stockton and San Francisco.[21] The latter was part of a massive project begun in 1914 to provide water to San Francisco from a dam and reservoir called the Hetch Hetchy in the mountains of eastern California.

In the early 1920s, the East Bay Municipal Utility District, which represented nine cities on the east side of San Francisco Bay, including

Thanks in large part to Charlie Shea's reputation for hard work, the J. F. Shea Company was able to win the $12 million contract for the Mokelumne Pipeline from the East Bay Municipal Utility District in California. It was the largest project the Sheas had undertaken. The pipeline was 65 inches in diameter, and the welded portion alone was more than 80 miles long.

Oakland and Berkeley, embarked on a project to bring water from the Mokelumne River in the Sierra Nevada mountain range across the great valley of central California and through the Berkeley Hills to the East Bay.

Although the job promised to be incredibly difficult, competition for the $12 million pipeline contract was stiff. It was coveted by many firms that were much better known in California than the J. F. Shea Company, including the Henry J. Kaiser and W. A. Bechtel companies, both of which would later partner with the Sheas as three of the fabled Six Companies that built the Hoover Dam.

Then and later, Charlie Shea's style was to outwork and outhustle the competition. The J. F. Shea Company might not be the biggest firm, but it was certainly one of the most aggressive and hardest working.

As former Shea employee Jack Garner recalled, "Charlie was sharp. He missed no bets. He found out where the competition was holed up bidding this project. He had one of his men go over there and stand in the hall to see how long they spent on that bid. All he wanted to know was how hard they were working to get it. When Charlie was told the lights went out at 2 A.M., he said, 'Oh, hell, we've got this job cinched.'"[22]

The bids were opened on September 4, 1925. To the surprise of Shea's

Charlie Shea had a sharp mind and competitive spirit. He was willing to go the extra mile to win bids.

competitors, the J. F. Shea Company won the contract in partnership with Twohy Brothers, which provided financial backing. Charlie would serve as general manager.

Perhaps the competition shouldn't have been surprised, however. As the *Encyclopedia of American Biography* noted, Charlie Shea "was famous for his prompt fulfillment of all contractual obligations, the reliability and high quality of his work and for his native honesty and fair dealing which led all who had relations with him to place implicit confidence in his assurances."[23]

The Mokelumne Pipeline was an enormous undertaking, easily the biggest project the Sheas had yet shouldered. As one writer observed, it is interesting to note that "the contract was secured while J. F. Shea was in Europe and without his knowledge, but—characteristic of his complete faith in his son's judgment—he never questioned Charlie's action."[24]

Nothing of the scope and difficulty of the Mokelumne Pipeline had ever taken shape in California before. The project was to consist mostly of welded steel pipe, with cement-lined tunnels to carry water through the Berkeley Hills. At the time, most pipelines were riveted. Although riveting was fast and cheap, some feared that a riveted pipeline of such enormous length would leak enough water annually to supply a city of 10,000 people. At the time, the next-largest acetylene-welded pipeline was 30 inches in diameter and less than 1,000 feet long.[25] By comparison, the Mokelumne

Pipeline was 65 inches in diameter and, even after subtracting the cement-lined tunnels and other nonpipeline intervals, ran on for more than 80 miles.[26]

The project seemed simple enough on paper. A 325-foot-high concrete dam (the Pardee Dam) would be built in the gorge at Lancha Plana in the Sierra Nevada. The dam would back up the Mokelumne River into a basin and create a reservoir covering almost 13,000 acres. When the reservoir reached a certain point above sea level, the water would be released into the pipeline and flow entirely by gravity down across the Central Valley to a point near Walnut Creek in the East San Francisco Bay area, where pumping stations would push the water on to the cities and newly built reservoirs of the East Bay.

Once the reservoir created by the Pardee Dam was filled, about 42 million gallons of water a day would flow continuously through the pipeline, a quarter of the Mokelumne River's flow. Including the pipeline, the dam, the reservoirs, and the various pumping stations, it was a $65 million project, paid for by bond issues.

In fact, the project wasn't that easy or straightforward, and no one really expected it to be. No job of this size ever was. First, construction of the dam was delayed. As a result, the pipeline was built to a nonexistent reservoir. With the fear of major water shortages looming in the rapidly growing East Bay cities, it was decided that the pipeline would temporarily draw the water directly from the Mokelumne River.

Using the usual process of the day, a low-carbon welding rod, Shea began acetylene welding of the pipeline in March 1926. The edges of the pipe were beveled to 45 degrees, and the welding was done entirely from the outside. Unfortunately, acetylene welding of an 80-mile pipeline proved to be impractical for a variety of reasons, including speed of assembly. About two dozen pipe sections were placed in position before "it became obvious that the difficulties were greater than anticipated."[27] Two months later, in May, riveting replaced welding, although

acetylene welding was used for the 26,000 feet of pipe that was already in the field and not provided with rivet holes.

The pipe itself had an inside diameter of 65 inches. The thickness of the pipe varied— its wall measured $\frac{3}{8}$ inch, $\frac{1}{2}$ inch, or $\frac{7}{8}$ inch, depending on conditions. The pipe was coated inside and out with special protective materials. In those days, electrolysis was a major problem for water lines. Metals in certain soils generated electrical currents that found their way into the pipe and traveled with the water until they located weak spots in the pipe's lining. Gradual nicking of the pipe eventually created holes and could endanger an entire pipeline. Consequently, "cathodic stations" were built along the way to divert currents into the ground. Also, as a precautionary measure, four giant valves were installed along the route. They would open automatically in case of a break in the pipeline and spill the water into nearby sloughs or ravines.

Huge trenching machines prepared the way, rooting a ditch eight feet wide and deep enough to bury the pipe under three to five feet in normal conditions. A traveling crane then lowered each 30-foot pipe section. On hillsides the pipe had to be anchored to prevent "creepage" once it was under pressure. In some areas the pipeline had to be carried above the ground on trestles.[28]

Probably the most difficult part of laying the pipeline came at the three river crossings because the pipe had to be placed several feet below the river bottoms. In the case of the San Joaquin River, where plans called for the channel to be deepened after the pipe was laid, the pipeline had to be at least 35 feet below the river bottom. Wrapped in steel fabric reinforcement and coated with gunite, with iron flanges for fastening under water, 120-foot sections of pipe were floated into place and sunk in cradles, there to rest on piles driven in a prepared trench. Divers then bolted the joints, which were encased in concrete, before the huge trench was backfilled.

Not long before, a typical water transport system in the West consisted of hollowed-out logs or pipes molded from primitive cast iron with such little flexibility that the conduits were too brittle for the job—which made the Mokelumne Pipeline an even more extraordinary undertaking. It was by far the most expensive pipeline built in California up to that time.

"This was the biggest experiment in the history of pipe laying," said E. L. MacDonald, one of the pipeline's project engineers.[29]

Like the J. F. Shea Company itself, the pipeline was a family operation. Gil Shea moved to California to run a portion of the work. Gil's wife, Lucile, gave birth to John F. Shea (company president since 1958) in Oakland in 1926. The baby's grandfather, John Francis Shea, lived with the family in Walnut Creek for several months.[30]

At the same time, to stay on top of the project as construction manager, Charlie Shea moved into San Francisco's Palace Hotel, which doubled as his home and headquarters. His wife, Lessie, and their four children went back to Portland after living briefly in San Francisco.[31] Charlie traveled by train back and forth between Portland and San Francisco, a trip that was said to be a "sleeper's night" long.

The Mokelumne Pipeline was a resounding success. At Lancha Plana, workmen knocked

down bulkheads to set the water flowing down the pipeline. All that night the water "moved like a liquid serpent" down the mountains, across the great valley, over the soft peat lands of the Sacramento Delta, through the hills, and into the Walnut Creek pumping station. At 4 P.M. on Sunday, June 23, 1929, the head of the stream dripped into the San Pablo Reservoir and began to spread.

Two thousand people gathered from the nine East Bay Municipal Utility District cities for a band concert, other entertainment, and speeches. A headline in the *Oakland Tribune* read "Water, Water Everywhere and Lots of It to Drink."[32] As one dignitary said, "The melting snows of the rugged peaks of Round Top Mountain are flowing down the Mokelumne River through the East Bay Aqueduct, past us here into the San Pablo Reservoir, and . . . into the distribution mains of the district. It is a day appropriate for music and poetry and imaginative expressions, rather than dry engineering facts."[33]

A Patriarch's Passing

While the Mokelumne Pipeline was a resounding triumph for the J. F. Shea Company and for Charlie Shea personally, it must have held a bittersweet quality, too. Less than a year after work on the pipeline began, on December 18, 1926, the company's founder, John Francis Shea, died at age 72 at his home on Johnson Street in Portland.

Although he had been ill, the patriarch's death shocked his family. In an interview 60 years later, daughter Dorothy Shea Murphy remembered being called home from a party when the end was near.

"I didn't realize he was deathly sick," she said. "We got a nurse and he died that night. It was very sudden, though the doctor said his heart was little more than tissue paper. He'd been to a movie with mother

This typical Shea warehouse in Portland was located on the south side of North Columbia Boulevard at the intersection with North Argyle Street.

and they stopped . . . for ice cream, and he had some pound cake and then they walked home from downtown—they used to really enjoy the walk. It was very sudden."[34]

John Francis Shea, who started with nothing but his own drive and ambition, the young man who risked his future on a long, hard journey from Ohio to California some 50 years earlier, left an estate valued at about $700,000, the equivalent of about $8 million today. His first-born son, Charlie, was appointed administrator of the estate.[35]

One person described John Francis Shea as a man who owed "his prosperity to tireless effort, good management and close conformity to a high standard of commercial ethics."[36] His Portland newspaper obituary praised him as a man who left his mark, "an active and well-known citizen, identified with the real physical growth of the city."[37]

His wife, Anna, outlived him by almost seven years. She died at the Hotel Del Coronado in San Diego on April 11, 1933.

Record Tunneling in Oregon

At about the same time the Mokelumne Pipeline project was winding down, the Sheas began work on their first major tunnel operations in Oregon.

Above: A family photo showing, from left: Lucile Shea (Gil Shea's wife and the mother of John F. Shea), Frank Shea, Mabel Shea, and Dorothy Shea Murphy (all children of John Francis and Anna Shea).

Right: Gilbert Shea, 12 years younger than his brother Charlie, began working at the family company as a boy. He attended college and at age 19 was allotted a 20 percent interest in the J. F. Shea Company.

One was a straightforward railroad tunnel built for the Union Pacific Railroad and completed in 1930. The second job was much more complex: two tunnels for the Federal Bureau of Reclamation's Owyhee Irrigation Project in eastern Oregon. The project's goal was to harness the wild Owyhee River and provide water to the remote Owyhee and Central Snake River Valleys of southeastern Oregon and southwestern Idaho, which included more than 120,000 acres of farmland.[38] The project would also help control floods. When the Owyhee Dam was completed in 1932, it was the world's tallest dam, a concrete-arch structure 417 feet high.[39]

The Sheas won two contracts totaling $1.6 million to build parts of two tunnels, together about five miles long, that would provide the main canal outlet. One concrete-lined tunnel was horseshoe-shaped and 16 feet 7 inches in diameter. The other concrete-lined tunnel was tubular and 9 feet 3 inches in diameter.[40]

Gil Shea was the on-site job supervisor. In Shea tradition, Gil already had extensive hands-on tunneling experience, including tunnel and pipeline work in Oakland and Portland, not to mention his lamplighting activity as a boy.

"He was small, but he was tough," recalled retired Shea employee Jack Garner many years later.[41] At one time Gil was considered one of the best "single jack" operators in the business. In the days before the jackhammer or air hammer, a man had to hold a drill in one hand and a sledge hammer in the other to make openings in the rock for explosives, a job that required the arm and shoulder strength of a blacksmith or a weight lifter.

Another perspective came from Philip Schuyler, editor of *Western Construction News.*

The Owyhee Irrigation Project in eastern Oregon diverted water from the Owyhee River to flow into the Owyhee and Central Snake River Valleys of southeastern Oregon and southwestern Idaho. The Sheas built parts of two tunnels that provided the main canal outlet. These photos show various aspects of Shea's work on the Owyhee tunnels: steel forms for lining one of the tunnels (opposite); sand and gravel loading at Shea's mixing plant (below); and a wide view of "Tunnel Canyon," which shows the compressor house and the concrete-mixing plant and placing equipment (bottom).

"[Gil Shea] has a winning personality and although very good natured and slight of build, he is hard to lick, as more than one man has found out."[42]

Gil Shea had to be tough. Tunneling was a tough job done by tough men in even tougher circumstances.

Shea's two Owyhee tunnels were driven simultaneously from one base camp. The 150-man camp included a mess house, a bunkhouse, a recreation hall, a commissary, and a bathhouse. Employees were charged $1.50 a day for board and lodging, $1.50 per month for medical services, and a penny a day for insurance.[43]

"Only the best grade of groceries, meats, etc., obtainable are served, and no better grub can be found in any other camp," Schuyler wrote. "It will be noted that there is no provision for women. This is strictly a he-man camp where even wives of the contractors, superintendent, office manager and foreman are taboo. Any man, no matter how valuable he is, who comes back to camp intoxicated from a jaunt

in town, is fired. . . . The result is that the men pretty generally refrain from sprees."[44]

Women were barred from the camp, but apparently children were permitted. Gil's young son John got his first exposure to tunnel work on the Owyhee job. Before he was old enough even to attend school, he remembered, he made several trips there with his father.[45]

In the larger of the two tunnels, each eight-hour shift consisted of 15 men, including "one shifter, four miners, four chuck tenders, one nipper, one mucking coreman, and four laborers." In the smaller tunnel, each shift required 13 men, only two of whom were laborers.[46]

The Sheas were known for paying excellent wages for the time. The shifters got $7 per eight-hour day, miners $6, chuck tenders and jackhammer operators $5. At the bottom of the wage scale were the underground laborers, who got

$4.50 per day, and the outside laborers, who were paid $4, solid pay in the 1930s.[47]

According to the Sheas' longtime attorney, Robert L. Bridges, the Sheas were highly respected employers. Even if a worker were offered a higher-paying job elsewhere, chances are he would choose the Sheas. "That was because of their reputation for professional supervision and good food on the camp jobs,"

Right: The J. F. Shea Co., Inc., completed the Owyhee tunnels in 1932, a year ahead of schedule. This railcar, according to one of the Shea crewmen, was "all that the Shea Co. left at the Owyhee job site."

Below: The Sheas instilled loyalty in their work crews and had a reputation for superior work supervision. This photo shows crewman Wallace Young with a Shea locomotive built to Shea's specified dimensions. *(From the collection of Margaret Young)*

Bridges said. "Few would turn down a Shea job to go elsewhere. No one treated people better than the Sheas."[48]

Another of Gil's sons, Gilbert, who chose to go into the securities business rather than construction, remembered how his father "always talked to us about honesty and not cheating. They did an awful lot of their business, up through the 1940s, just on a handshake deal."[49]

Dorothy Murphy (not to be confused with Dorothy Shea Murphy), whose husband, Peter Murphy, worked under Gil, described Gil as "a dedicated boss and very smart. He took care of the men."[50]

In 1931 the Shea Owyhee crew broke two world records for tunnel excavation by completing 1,315 feet of tunnel in 31 days and 63 feet in one day. Even when records weren't being set,

the job moved fast. The Owyhee tunnels were completed in 1932, a year earlier than projected.[51]

Organization, innovation, and a little luck were the main reasons for the speedy pace. For example, the blasted material was hauled out of the tunnels on railroad cars pulled by gas locomotives, which were large and efficient. Because of the danger from exhaust fumes, it was unusual for gas locomotives to operate so deep underground. The Sheas were fortunate that the rock contained no natural gases that could be ignited. Also, the ventilation system was carefully designed to keep the tunnels free from powder and exhaust fumes, and each locomotive was equipped with a special water tank that absorbed much of the carbon monoxide from the gas engines.[52]

The Sheas also made significant on-the-job improvements in the excavating equipment. Dubbed "Owyhee-type muckers," the exca-

vating tools were later used widely throughout the industry.

Another strategy that helped move construction along was the use of new "Atlas-Giant No. 8 all-metal delay fuses." The fuses ensured simultaneous explosion of each series of holes, which resulted "in full effectiveness of each charge and a consolidation of the blasted rock." Ten minutes before a round was shot, the blowers were reversed and the powder gases sucked out rather than being driven back into the tunnel.[53]

But more than all of that, leadership and efficiency pulled everything together and made the operation work as well as it did.

"Every operation, including setting of timbers, is nicely timed, Schuyler wrote. "It is a case of feverish activity with hardly an interval of delay, every man having a particular job to perform. There is no driving of the men, the different shifts becoming imbued with the spirit

The Henry Building served as Shea's final headquarters in Portland before the company relocated to California. *(Photo courtesy Oregon Historical Society)*

of competition, together with the desire to beat previous records."[54]

Looking to California

Despite his brother's successful activity in Oregon, Charlie Shea increasingly cast his eyes toward California, which offered more opportunities and larger construction projects.

"After my father's death, Charlie called me one day and said, 'Dot, I'd like to have you come see me in my office,'" recalled Charlie's youngest sister, Dorothy Shea Murphy.[55]

The meeting took place in the Henry Building in Portland, which was still the official headquarters of the J. F. Shea Company despite the fact that, for all practical purposes, Charlie no longer lived in Portland.[56]

"I went down to the office, and he said, 'There's no chance of making money in Portland.'" Charlie told his sister he wanted to move the company's headquarters to California "and get in with somebody big. . . . There's no future here," he told her. "There's no big business."[57]

Another perspective came from a 1934 letter to the Oregon State Tax Commission written on behalf of Charlie Shea by Earl L. Fisher, an attorney with the Portland law firm of Lewis, Lewis & Finnigan. The letter explained that after Charlie's father, John Francis Shea, died in 1926, the estate was probated, and all of the father's business affairs were fully closed two years later. "Since that time, all business ties of Charles A. Shea in the state of Oregon ceased," Fisher wrote. "In the year 1928 Mr. Shea definitely decided to establish his residence and domicile in the state of California. . . . Since 1928 Mr. Shea has not been in the State of Oregon more than ten days out of the year."[58]

The letter went on to say that after John Francis Shea's death, the company had been reorganized and incorporated in Delaware as the J. F. Shea Co., Inc., with brothers Charlie, Gil, and Ed Shea retaining a majority interest, although the rest of the family had an interest, too.[59]

In the meantime, the company was associated with "many large contracting projects" in California, Nevada, Arizona, and elsewhere, with only three contracts in Oregon during this time, including the Union Pacific tunnel job and the Owyhee irrigation project. Fisher explained that virtually all of Charlie Shea's professional ties were in California and that he served on several boards of directors, all of which met in San Francisco. He was also a member of San Francisco's prestigious Olympic Club.[60] "Mr. Shea has established a permanent address at the Palace Hotel, San Francisco, where his personal belongings, clothing and other effects are located," Fisher added, noting that Charlie's wife lived in Portland to be closer to their grandchildren.[61]

There was no doubt about it; although Shea would continue to work and build all around the country, its future lay in California.

Charlie Shea (far right) stands before the Hoover Dam construction site. To build the mighty Hoover Dam, the J. F. Shea Company joined a partnership called the Six Companies.

CHAPTER THREE

HELPING TO BUILD HISTORY

1931–1935

The National Reclamation Act conjured up, like some glittering grail of future prosperity, a vision of dams and aqueducts bejeweling the country's unwatered tracts.

—historian Edmund Morris,
on President Theodore Roosevelt's
signing the National Reclamation Act into law in 1902

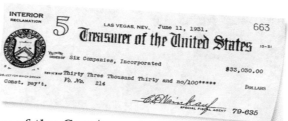

THE J. F. SHEA Company was uniquely positioned during the long years of the Great Depression. While most other companies suffered from the deep recessionary economy, Shea reaped the financial benefits of taking on some of the country's most challenging construction projects. Hoover Dam, the Golden Gate Bridge, and the San Francisco–Oakland Bay Bridge were not only difficult to build, but each became a historical landmark. All three projects advanced Shea's already solid reputation as a premier contractor.

Dam Complications

It is generally assumed that Hoover Dam was the result of President Franklin D. Roosevelt's New Deal, a massive public works program in the 1930s launched with a hefty push from the federal government to help America work its way out of the Great Depression. Hoover Dam, easily the most spectacular construction feat of the Depression years, was indeed a boon to employment; as many as 5,000 men worked at the construction site at one time, and the ripples from that employment were felt far and wide.

But Roosevelt's plan for the federal government to spend the country back to prosperity didn't begin until 1933, one year after his election, two years after work on the dam got under way, and four years after the stock market crash of 1929 triggered the start of the Great Depression.

Plans that would ultimately turn into Hoover Dam had been in the works for decades. During the Theodore Roosevelt administration (1901–1909), Arthur Powell Davis, head of the newly formed U.S. Bureau of Reclamation, proposed the idea of damming the Colorado River.[1] Even before that, explorer and naturalist John Wesley Powell was one of many who urged the construction of huge irrigation systems to collect and distribute western floodwaters.

Davis couldn't be accused of thinking small. He wanted to develop the Colorado River

---

On June 11, 1931, the Six Companies received its first payment from the government for work on Hoover Dam, a check in the amount of $33,030. The check was copied and saved as a souvenir by Six Companies member E. O. Wattis.

time when travel was exceedingly difficult. For example, during that time a flight from San Francisco to Los Angeles took two hours, while today it takes one hour.

All-Around Success

Although work on the diversion tunnels moved at a rapid pace, the labor was miserable. But finally—18 months and three floods after the first blasting began—the tunnels were completed.

Two massive earthen cofferdams—watertight temporary caissons used to keep water out of an area where a permanent dam is to be built—were erected to seal off the site's foundation. Swarms of men and machines moved in to remove hundreds of feet of accumulated silt and debris to expose the bedrock.

On June 6, 1933, the first 16-ton bucket of concrete swung down from the canyon rim to be emptied into a house-size wooden form, the first of more than 200 forms that would be used on the dam. The ritual would continue at the rate of one bucket of concrete per minute. If the dam had been poured solid, it would have taken 125 years to dry, and the enormous pressures exerted on it by its own bulk would have raised the internal temperatures of the concrete so high as to warp or crack it. As the dam grew, special tubing filled with water was inserted into the cement to cool it in summer and heat it in winter to prevent excessive expansion and contraction.

By most accounts, the Six Companies knew it was financially in the clear before the first year of work ended. In making its bid, it reportedly shaved the estimate on concrete and other items while inflating the excavation costs. One source says that a reasonable price for the excavation work would have been $5 or $6 per cubic yard. The Six Companies bid it at $8.50. Since the bulk of the excavation costs came at an early stage with the building of the diversion tunnels, the Six Companies took its profit early. The technique, called an "unbalanced bid," would become common practice in the construction field.[50] The Six Companies gained as much as $6 million in profits before it poured the first concrete for the dam, meaning that it got back all of the $5 million put up initially, plus another $1 million.[51]

Although the dam wasn't finished until 1935, a remarkable two full years ahead of schedule, it was Shea's opinion that the hard work was already done with the building of the tunnels. "From Charlie's point of view it was licked . . . [in] 1933 because the excavation was complete," Bridges said. "The rest of it was just pouring concrete. The excavation of the tunnels was the difficult part."[52]

While the Six Companies engaged in building Hoover Dam, construction business elsewhere was booming, and the J. F. Shea Company was well positioned to reap the benefits. Around the same time as the Hoover Dam project got under way, Shea became involved in building another lasting landmark: the Golden Gate Bridge.

The Golden Gate Bridge

Well into the 1930s, travel to and from San Francisco was done primarily by ferry. The only way to reach the city by car was from the south San Francisco Bay area through San Jose. From Marin County to the north and from Oakland to the east, San Francisco, one of the nation's largest and most interesting cities, could be reached only by water.

The bridge across the "Golden Gate" entrance from the Pacific Ocean to San Francisco Bay got its start when the Golden Gate Bridge and Highway District was formed in 1928. Two years later, despite the onslaught of the Great Depression, voters enthusiastically approved a $35 million bond

---

Opposite: Hoover Dam was completed in 1935, two years ahead of schedule. The colossal structure straddles the Colorado River and reaches into both Arizona and Nevada.

This page and opposite: The J. F. Shea Company and Pacific Bridge built the piers and abutments for the famous Golden Gate Bridge, which spans the "Golden Gate" strait from the Pacific Ocean to San Francisco Bay. When completed it was the longest suspension bridge in the world.

Building the Golden Gate Bridge was extremely difficult in a number of ways. For example, the pier on the San Francisco side was erected in water depths of more than 100 feet amid churning tides of five to seven knots. Shifting winds, thick fog, and harsh storms also plagued workers.

issue to finance the bridge and its complex approaches. A call for bids was issued on June 17, 1931.

The design called for a single-span bridge of 4,200 feet from tower center to tower center, which made it the longest suspension bridge in the world for many years. Allowing for cable sag of 475 feet, navigational clearance of 220 feet, and several other factors, the tower heights were set at 746 feet above the water. Side spans of 1,125 feet each connected the structure with 9,000 feet of roadway through the Presidio in San Francisco and with 5,200 feet of road on the Marin County side.[53]

Aside from the sheer size of such a span, the Golden Gate Bridge posed unique problems. The bridge had to be anchored deep enough to withstand ferocious tides and waves and bear its roadway high enough for oceangoing ships to pass beneath it at high tide. It also had to resist the fierce winds of San Francisco Bay. The towers would have to sustain an enormous top load while resting on a relatively narrow base. Adding to the design concerns, the bridge was to be located only 12 miles from the San Andreas Fault.

Bethlehem Steel won the contract to build the bridge itself, and a joint venture between the J. F. Shea Company, represented by Ed Shea, and Pacific Bridge, represented by Jack Graham, won the $3.6 million contract to build the bridge's piers and abutments. (A pier is a heavy structure that supports the spans of the bridge, and an abutment supports either end span of a long bridge.) The vertical load on each pier would weigh in at almost 165 million pounds, with 44 feet of each pier above sea level and approximately 100 feet below. The area at the base would measure 80 feet by 160 feet. The area at the top would be 65 feet by 140 feet.[54] Never before in bridge building had foundations been laid so deep.[55]

Henry Kaiser brought in his own group to bid against Shea and Pacific Bridge. Kaiser lost but shifted his interest to another area and wound up winning the contract to build the approach structures at both ends of the bridge.

The Golden Gate Bridge was an excruciatingly difficult construction job. Several of those involved say it was the most difficult of their careers.[56] The pier on the San Francisco side was located in water more than 100 feet deep and 1,125 feet from shore amid swirling tides of five to seven knots.[57] The crews also faced constantly shifting winds, blinding fog, and the frequent, violent storms that are characteristic of San Francisco Bay.

The building of the Golden Gate Bridge was also notable for several firsts in heavy construction. For the first time, strict safety standards for dress were policy; it was the first major job on which hard hats were required, for example. Also, the job was the first to use trucks that mixed as well as carried concrete.

Although Charlie Shea was still spending most of his time at Hoover Dam, he had kept his hotel residence in San Francisco. The Six Companies' board meetings usually were held in San Francisco, too. As a result, Charlie often visited the Golden Gate Bridge construction site, especially during the more difficult stages.

"He'd come down at five every morning," recalled his sister, Dorothy Shea Murphy. "He'd have his chauffeur take him to about three blocks from the project, and he'd get out and walk because he didn't want to appear with his car and chauffeur."[58]

Though Charlie Shea made frequent appearances at the job site, Ed Shea supervised the bulk of the work. On the Marin County side, Ed oversaw the difficult and dangerous job of sinking the deepest cement piers and largest concrete abutments ever poured at that time. For the sake of convenience, his family lived nearby, in Sausalito. Once the Marin side was finished, Ed Shea began work on the San Francisco side, so his family moved to San Francisco. Like most builders in those days, the Sheas lived where the work was.

Ed Shea (above and right), the youngest brother of Charlie Shea, supervised most of Shea's work on the Golden Gate Bridge.

While the bridge's north pier was finished in only 101 days, the south pier turned out to be extraordinarily—almost catastrophically—difficult.[59]

Five months into the job, a steamer went off course in the Bay Area fog and crashed into an access trestle, destroying it. Four months later, divers discovered that blasting operations had shattered some of the rock on which the pier was to rest. It became necessary to penetrate another 35 feet into the ocean's rock bottom to create acceptable support. The south pier ultimately took almost two years to complete, and the bridge finally opened in 1937.

Another Bridge on the Bay

As if Shea wasn't busy enough with Hoover Dam, the Golden Gate Bridge, and other projects, it was also a member of the Transbay Construction Company, which in 1933 was awarded a $7 million contract to build the west substructure of the San Francisco–Oakland Bay Bridge.

Transbay, which defeated a rival group led once again by Henry Kaiser, was a joint venture of Shea, MacDonald & Kahn, Pacific Bridge, General Construction, and Morrison-Knudsen. Transbay won the contract to build a portion of the 1.8-mile western section of the bridge between San Francisco and Yerba Buena Island. As had happened with the Golden Gate Bridge project, Kaiser's group went on to win another contract, this one to build from Yerba Buena Island to Oakland.

The Bay Bridge is the longest steel high-level bridge in the world. One of its piers sits 246 feet below water and required more concrete to build than the Empire State Building.

The Bay Bridge was a "double-decker," with one level for automobile traffic and another for trucks and rapid transit tracks. Shea and Pacific Bridge built the foundations, including four main-tower anchor blocks and the center anchor block, which required the deepest foundation ever laid,[60] plus deeper and taller bridge piers than had ever been built. One of the piers had to go down 246 feet to bedrock, a record at the time. When one of the huge piers began to tip, a situation that would have been disastrous, divers spurted jets of compressed air under the immense structure to right it.

Some of the most difficult work involved sinking caissons as big as football fields. (A caisson is a watertight enclosure inside which construction work can be done under water.) After attending a black-tie function in San Francisco, several of the partners, including Charlie Shea, gathered at the construction site's ferry building in the middle of the night. Still formally dressed, they looked out at the largest caisson ever built, dangling above San Francisco Bay. As they gazed at the caisson, one of the men finally broke the silence. "We'll either be broke tomorrow, or we will be very successful contractors." Fortunately, the caisson came down within an eighth of an inch of its target,[61] saving the partners from going broke.

Repositioning

On May 9, 1932, the partnership among Charlie, Ed, and Gil Shea that formed the J. F. Shea Company was dissolved in favor of the Delaware-incorporated J. F. Shea Co., Inc. The holdings were divided among the family members, although Charlie Shea retained the lion's share of the capital stock.

The following year brought another change. Until then, Shea's headquarters had been located in Portland, although in reality the headquarters was wherever the Sheas happened to be working. In 1933 the Sheas moved the business offices south to the

This stock certificate represents a portion of the Sheas' interest in Transbay Construction, a joint venture that built the San Francisco–Oakland Bay Bridge.

Oviatt Building at Sixth and Olive in Los Angeles. The old art deco building was built in 1928 and is listed in the National Register of Historic Places.[62]

The Shea brothers were scattered all over the West. Charlie was still supervising the construction of Hoover Dam in Nevada. Ed, his wife, Margaret, and their family (including future Shea vice presidents Ed and Peter) were living in the San Francisco area, where Ed was working on the Golden Gate Bridge. By then Gil and his wife, Lucile, had moved with their family (including future company president John F. Shea) to Los Angeles to begin work on the Los Angeles aqueduct for the Metropolitan Water District (MWD). This was the first of many projects Shea would perform for the MWD and the primary reason for the company's move to Los Angeles.[63]

For the Sheas, a new era was about to begin.

As part of the Six Companies joint venture, Shea played a huge role in construction of Parker Dam, designed to divert water from the Colorado River into the Los Angeles Aqueduct.

THE AGE OF GIANTS

1934–1942

By the time war broke across Poland in 1939, the Six Companies, that confederation of resolute, risk-taking western contractors, were more than ready for the tasks that history was preparing for them.

—*Fortune* magazine, "The Earth Movers," 1943

WHEN FRANKLIN DELANO Roosevelt entered the White House in 1933, the country was in the midst of the worst economic collapse in U.S. history. Thousands of banks had closed, farmers had lost their land, homeowners had lost their homes, and workers were without jobs.

In his inaugural speech, Roosevelt promised to ask Congress for "broad executive power to wage a war against the emergency, as great a power that would be given to me if we were in fact to be invaded."[1]

Roosevelt's strategy came to be known as the New Deal, the innovative and sometimes controversial series of measures adopted to break the back of the Great Depression. Basically the New Deal was an unprecedented array of subsidies—massive federal spending with the aim of generating purchasing power at the consumer level to lift the country out of the Depression. These programs included major capital distribution from the federal government to the states, extensive public works programs, production-control programs to raise prices in agriculture, and various programs of debt relief and consumer protection. Some of the organizations created by the New Deal included the Federal Emergency Relief Administration, which funneled tens of millions of dollars from the federal government to the states; the Civilian Conservation Corps, which put thousands of young men to work in a quasi-military setting; the Tennessee Valley Authority, which developed the Tennessee River to improve navigation and provide flood control and electric power to vast regions of the Southeast; and the Public Works Administration, which created a series of federally funded construction and utilities projects.

One result of the New Deal was an explosion of large-scale government-funded construction unlike anything the nation had seen. This "vast program of public works" included "a whole series of . . . dams." The names resonate today: Bonneville and Grand Coulee on the Columbia River; Shasta on the Sacramento River; and Parker Dam, 155 miles downriver of

---

In 1933, President Franklin D. Roosevelt visits a Civilian Conservation Corps (CCC) camp in Virginia's Shenandoah Valley. Roosevelt's New Deal instituted a number of public works programs such as the CCC. *(Photo courtesy National Archives)*

John, Edmund, and Peter Shea all worked on the Clear Creek Tunnel. The project began in 1957.

CHAPTER FIVE

WAR AND RENEWAL

1941–1958

By the late 1950s, Shea had reestablished itself as a major contender in heavy construction . . . [and] regained a position of dominance in tunnel work.

—historian Donald E. Wolf, *Big Dams and Other Dreams: The Six Companies Story*

THE JAPANESE ATTACK ON Pearl Harbor on December 7, 1941—only seven weeks before Charlie Shea's death—brought profound changes to the company and to the nation.

One of the changes raises the question of what might have been. A Shea-Kaiser joint venture was the low bidder on a project to increase the size and capacity of the Panama Canal. At the time, Ed Shea and his family were living in New York while Ed worked on a Shea-Kaiser joint venture on the Delaware Aqueduct and prepared to move to Panama for the canal project. When it was canceled as a result of the war, the plan to relocate to Panama was abandoned, and Ed and his family eventually moved back to California.[1]

After Charlie's death, Gil Shea became president of the company, overseeing several heavy construction jobs already in progress. However, the War Production Board considered dams, tunnels, and highways a low priority, and virtually all of Shea's major projects either slowed or stopped as men and material were diverted to the war effort, a situation that didn't change until well after the war ended in 1945.

Wartime Priorities

Sometimes it was simply impossible to get material. Responding to a Shea request for truck tires, Harry K. Martin, of Firestone Tires, wrote, "I wish to inform you that the prospects of furnishing you a quantity of large size truck tires in the immediate future are practically nil. . . . Nearly all available tire builders are used in the production of tires for the military."[2]

In another case, replying to Shea's request for equipment for a U.S. Bureau of Reclamation canal project in Southern California's Coachella Valley, L. J. Gardella, district chief of the Construction Machinery Division of the War Production Board, replied, "This office regrets to inform you that the equipment which you have applied for on and off in the past several months have [*sic*] been denied. . . . We regret very much that we could not have been of some service to you and can not make any definite commitment to you as to the future. Used equipment—

The Clear Creek Tunnel is nine miles long and moves water from the Trinity River in northern California to the Whiskeytown Reservoir.

When completed in 1953, Hungry Horse Dam on the south fork of the Flathead River in northwest Montana became the fourth-largest concrete dam in the world and the fourth-highest. The dam plays a major role in producing power for the Pacific Northwest. *(Photo courtesy Bureau of Reclamation)*

two months later his thigh was severely
bruised by flying rock from a tunnel portaling
blasting operation.

At the conclusion of Big Cliff, Edmund
Shea, having finished his tour of duty in the air
force, joined John in the business. They proceeded to successfully bid and construct two
concrete reservoirs, one in Altadena, California,
for $40,000, and one in Burbank, California,
for $500,000. Then during 1955, the Shea
Company was the low bidder on the Hills Creek
Diversion tunnel in Oregon for the Corps of
Engineers. This was a major project for the relatively inexperienced John and Edmund.[34]

Clear Creek Tunnel

In 1956, after finishing the supervision of
Hills Creek, which turned out to be a great

Above and right: Work on the Clear Creek Tunnel was
particularly challenging. Water often flooded the tunnel,
and the project was perilously close to San Andreas Fault
lines that ran through the earth.

In 1966, Shea won the contract for the $100 million Angeles Tunnel, the largest tunneling contract up to that time.

CHAPTER SIX

NEW HORIZONS

1958–1971

Tunnel building had been a staple for Shea, . . . and it became one again.

—historian Donald E. Wolf, *Big Dams and Other Dreams:*
The Six Companies Story

ON MARCH 26, 1958, A NEW company—J. F. Shea Co., Inc.—was born. It was owned and operated by a third generation of Sheas: John Shea, the son of Gil Shea, was president; his two cousins, Edmund and Peter Shea, both sons of Ed Shea, were vice presidents. At the time, John and Ed had just married and were both living in Redding, and Peter was still in school at Berkeley.

Like their fathers before them, John, Peter, and Edmund were raised in the business. John's first memory of his family's construction business is the Owyhee Tunnel job in eastern Oregon in the early 1930s, when he was only about five years old.

"I stayed in camp with my dad," he recalled. "Almost every day I would go to a little place away from the camp where I could look down on the portal of the tunnel and watch them haul the muck out. I'd just sit there and watch."[1]

For legal reasons, the name of the company was changed from the Shea Company to J. F. Shea Co., Inc., but the company itself—the operations and traditions that dated back to 1881—remained unchanged. "There have been three Shea companies, but it's always been the same, with each company succeeding the

prior one," explained Edmund Shea. "It's the same family and the same organization."[2]

Though J. F. Shea Co., Inc., was capitalized for just $160,000 (the equivalent of about $1 million in 2003), it enjoyed some important benefits. The older generation passed on its construction expertise and bonding capacity. Moreover, the younger generation inherited a number of relationships that continued to prove fruitful for the Sheas, including relationships with Morrison-Knudsen, Kaiser, and Macco Construction. "These relationships by themselves didn't give us any advantage over the competition," explained Edmund, "but it helped with bonding and financial capacity in bidding multimillion-dollar projects. We were able to bid and manage these large projects."[3]

The new company was fortunate to lose one of its first bids. As a 5 percent joint venture partner with Kaiser Engineers and

By the late 1960s, Peter Shea, vice president, had overseen a number of projects in heavy construction. He would later become president of Shea's construction division.

Macco Construction, Shea bid on an Army Corps of Engineers dam project in Bend, Oregon. Shea's joint venture narrowly lost the bid and was $7 million below the next bidder. The company that won the bid, Utah Construction, ended up losing a significant amount of money on the job. Even with only a 5 percent interest in the joint venture, Shea's loss would have been more than its net worth and would have wiped out the company. "After that experience," said Edmund, "we wanted to make sure we sponsored the work or else were very careful about who our partners were going to be."

At the time of the transition from one generation to the next, Shea kept its headquarters in Redding, California, where John's four oldest children and Edmund's four oldest were born. Most of Shea's jobs were in Northern California during the early 1960s. They included the Clear Creek Tunnel project, the Pit-McCloud Tunnel, and considerable work on the interstate highway system. Shea would stay involved with construction of the interstate highway system well into the 21st century.

Building the Nation's Highways

Although Americans take it for granted today, the interstate highway system was a revolutionary project. It changed the nation's lifestyle, was vital to the rise of suburbia, and connected the various sections of a sprawling country in a way that would otherwise have been impossible.

"Together, the united forces of our communication and transportation systems are dynamic elements in the very name we bear—United States," declared President Dwight D. Eisenhower. "Without them we would be a mere alliance of many parts."[4]

In 1956 Eisenhower signed the Federal-Aid Highway Act, which authorized construction of more than 41,000 miles of high-quality highways to link the nation, but America's history of highway construction goes back many years before that.

In 1919, when Eisenhower was a young U.S. Army lieutenant, he volunteered to accompany the first transcontinental motor convoy from Washington, D.C., to San Francisco. In an era of rough travel over unpaved roads (when there were any roads at all), the rigorous cross-country trip took the convoy 62 days.[5]

As he rose in the ranks, Eisenhower remembered the grueling experience. Many years later, during World War II, General Eisenhower, supreme commander of the Allied forces in Europe, was impressed with the fast and well-maintained German autobahn network. He later wrote, "The old convoy had started me thinking about good two-lane highways, but Germany made me see the wisdom of broader ribbons across the land."[6]

President Franklin D. Roosevelt was interested in improving America's roads, too. In the 1930s, at the height of the Great Depression, Roosevelt urged building a series of toll superhighways across the country. In addition to enhancing national transportation, Roosevelt saw the project as a way of providing jobs for an out-of-work America.[7]

World War II put the plan on hold. It was not until 11 years after the war ended, in fact, that Eisenhower signed the Federal-Aid Highway Act, which authorized the national network of high-quality highways officially known as the Dwight D. Eisenhower System of Interstate and Defense Highways.

Over the years, Shea played an impressive role in building and maintaining the interstate highway system, which has been cited as one of the 20th century's top 10 construction achievements, along with two other Shea projects, the Golden Gate Bridge and Hoover Dam.

First as a supplier and then as contractor, J. F. Shea Redding provided much of the work and material for the construction and rehabilitation of Interstate 5 from Red Bluff, California, to the Oregon border. In the 1960s the Redding aggregate plants provided material for the portion of Interstate 5 at the Sacramento River in northern California. J. F. Shea Redding also provided the asphalt for that section's shoulders and ramps.[8]

A Heavy Competitor

One of the new generation of Sheas' greatest accomplishments was to reestablish the company "as a major contender in heavy construction. Tunnel building had been a staple for Shea," wrote Six Companies historian Donald E. Wolf, ". . . and it became one again." In fact, the J. F. Shea Co., Inc., assumed a position of dominance in the field.[9]

The 1960s continued successfully with a series of public works projects that frequently brought Shea back in contact with one or another of its old Six Companies partners, sometimes as a competitor and sometimes as a partner.

John Shea was project manager and Peter was assistant project manager and general superintendent on the four tunnels for Northern

The new generation of Sheas reinvigorated the company's work in heavy construction. Seated, from left: Peter Shea, John Shea, and Edmund Shea. Pictured in paintings, from left: John F. Shea, Charlie Shea, Gil Shea, and Ed Shea.

In 1966 Shea won a contract for the Angeles Tunnel for more than $100 million, touted as the largest tunneling contract at that time. The Angeles Tunnel was yet another part of the California Aqueduct and helped bring water from northern California through the Tehachapi Mountains to Southern California. With a diameter of 35 feet, the extraordinary size of the 7.2-mile tunnel allowed Shea to drill the upper half for the entire length and then excavate the lower half. More than 100 million pounds of steel and almost 500,000 cubic yards of concrete were used on the Angeles Tunnel.[12]

Mike Shank was project manager for the Angeles Tunnel and also bid and managed the intake works at Angeles Tunnel. He later was project manager for Pyramid Dam and Crystal Dam. Shank proved his abilities on each project and was instrumental in enhancing the growth of the J. F. Shea Co. He then retired from Shea and started his own successful construction business.

Also during this period, Shea constructed the five-mile San Bernardino Tunnel in Southern California for the Department of Water Resources, with Dick Roberts as project manager.

With so much work going on in Southern California, in 1969 the Sheas settled into new corporate offices in Walnut, named the Shea Center, where they could oversee their growing group of divisions and subsidiaries. Until that time, they typically worked out of trailers at their job sites. Though they had an official headquarters office, their functional headquarters had been wherever they happened to be working.

The BART System

In 1965 Edmund Shea, who had been in Redding running Shea Sand and Gravel and bidding local highway work, relocated to Berkeley, California. Dick Rowan then became general manager of Redding, reporting to Edmund, and Edmund became area manager for six joint ventures (and was also project manager for three of the six) to build the

Bay Area Rapid Transit (BART) system, which links Oakland and the East San Francisco Bay area with the city of San Francisco. Shea won a good share of the work and was, in fact, the first contractor to work on the BART system.[13] It was while working on the BART projects that Edmund's two youngest children were born in Oakland, California.

The largest of the six projects, the Berkeley Hills Tunnel, was a joint venture of Shea, Kaiser Industries Corporation, and Macco Construction. The partners had submitted a low bid of $30.9 million[14] for what was actually twin tunnels, each 3.2 miles long.

The *Engineering News Record* stated that the twin tunnels "will be one of the longest and most expensive railroad tunnels built in the U.S. in recent years." It also predicted that "rapid transit construction will be big business in the San Francisco Bay area during the next few years. . . . [T]ransit officials estimate that about 100 contracts totaling $625 million will be required to complete the system."[15]

The Berkeley Hills Tunnel was a difficult project, "a seismic nightmare with over 200 soil changes," as one magazine observed, plus stretches of propane and methane gas.[16] A day's excavation progress varied from as little as two feet to 38 feet.[17]

The Ashby Tunnel on the BART project required something of a learning curve. "I think Ashby was the first soft-ground tunnel the new generation of Sheas had ever done," said Bill Morris, who at the time was part of the joint venture as an employee of Macco.[18] (Morris later joined Shea.)

Despite the learning curve, the job was a success, and the contract was completed in 425 working days. According to Morris, the

Opposite: Shea joint ventured on six Bay Area Rapid Transit (BART) system projects in the San Francisco area. Edmund Shea was regional manager for all six. The Berkeley Hills Tunnel was the largest and involved two 3.2-mile railroad tunnels.

Above: Approaches to the Berkeley North Subway, one of the BART projects. Construction of the Berkeley Hills Tunnel was memorable for a great variety of geological problems. The tunnels plunged through miles of fault-augered sandstone, shale, chert, conglomerate, basalt, coal, and other materials—more than 200 soil changes in all—and also encountered stretches of petroleum and methane gas.

Right: The completed BART system linked Oakland and the East San Francisco Bay area with the city of San Francisco.

Shea-Macco joint venture became the first company to install steel liner plates (11,000 in all) for the BART project. The 16-foot-diameter steel plates had been manufactured for the project by Kaiser Steel a few years before the start of construction. "The engineers didn't know whether those steel plates were going to work," Morris said. "We had some problems erecting the plates at first, but once we learned how to do it, we were off and running."[19]

Another of Shea's joint venture BART projects was the Powell Street subway station, under San Francisco's Market Street, one of the busiest urban centers in the world. Buck Atherton was the project manager for the $27 million project, which had to be done without disturbing the traffic and pedestrians above.

The job went smoothly. According to long-time Shea associate Merv Koster, "It is a tunnel-driving custom that when there is a holing-through meeting, whether it is from opposite directions or the end of a one-way line, the contractor hosts a 'holing-through' party where all friends and associates are invited. In this instance the party was held on the train entrance and departure ramps. The overhead traffic on Market Street could be heard but the party was a merry one and without one interruption."[20]

New Horizons

The decade of the 1970s presented a difficult time for the American economy and businesses in general. The escalating Vietnam War, a political climate that was increasingly rife with environmental concerns, foreign competition, and a lack of underground tunnel work "contributed to a slowing trend in construction, and it became important for Shea to diversify," said Edmund Shea.[21]

The continuing success of Shea's heavy construction business gave the company the financial base to broaden its activities. So while many businesses remained stagnant or worse in the floundering economy, the J. F. Shea Co., Inc., would master new technologies and techniques and diversify into new endeavors, including venture capital, homebuilding, and property development.

Shea Homes offers a broad spectrum of homes in California, Arizona, Colorado, and North Carolina. Pictured are the interior and exterior of Verranzzano, near San Diego.

CHAPTER SEVEN

SHEA HOMES

1968–2004

Because we had capital reserves from the tunnel business, we were looking at other business opportunities. Then John McCloud encouraged us to go into homebuilding, and that's what we did.

—John F. Shea,
President

SHEA'S MOST SIGNIFICANT diversification was its July 3, 1968, entry into homebuilding with the creation of PBS Corporation, the predecessor of Shea Homes. When it began, PBS had only six employees, all in Newport Beach, California. But by the end of its first year, it had 145 homes under construction, plus land acquisition in the Southern California cities of Santa Ana, Fountain Valley, Sylmar, Cerritos, and Huntington Beach.

Though in 1962 John and Edmund Shea had bought about 500 acres in Redding, California, John said they sold the land in 1970 "because it tied up too much money. It was a pure speculation that accrued a small positive margin."[1] According to John, the company didn't even consider going into the homebuilding business until 1968.[2] "We were able to go into homebuilding because of our financial success in the tunnel business," he said.[3]

The idea was proposed to the Sheas by John McCloud of Macco Construction. Shea and Macco had a history of successful joint ventures, including the Clear Creek, Pit-McCloud, and BART projects. McCloud had recently sold his homebuilding business to Pennsylvania Railroad. Two of his top men,

John Parker and Glen Brengle, were hired to run the new operation for the railroad. However, they were not happy there, so on their behalf, McCloud contacted Edmund Shea to suggest that the Sheas might be interested in entering the homebuilding field.

According to John Shea, the partners agreed that the Sheas would finance the business and that Parker and Brengle would run it. The firm's name came from the initials of the three principals: Parker, Brengle, and Shea.[4]

Parker and Brengle each owned 7 percent of PBS Corporation, and the J. F. Shea Co., Inc., owned the remaining 86 percent. "We put up practically all the money," said John Shea. "Ed, Peter, and I didn't know anything about homebuilding, but Parker and Brengle knew a lot about it. They had options to buy land in Huntington Beach, Cerritos, and Santa Ana, so we bought these properties and immediately got started building homes."[5]

The Silver Creek Valley Country Club is part of a master-planned community in San Jose, California.

removed from the average person who comes into the company," he said.[11]

　　Shea Homes' relatively slow growth in the 1970s was due in part to the fact that the company was still finding its way in the home-

Shea Homes Arizona offers a wide range of beautiful homes such as Avante at Cooper Corners East (left) and Enclaves del Norte at Seville (bottom). The Seville master-planned community includes an 18-hole golf course (center), a community center, and other recreational activities.

building field. "The business had much more of a construction mentality in the early seventies," Humphreys said. "The heads of companies came out of the construction side, and that was sort of the realm of the company. I think the business has changed dramatically in that way."[12]

As Shea Homes evolved, it became more diversified, and its people became experts in areas such as finance, marketing, sales, and design. As Humphreys observed, "Companies today have to be much more rounded," and Shea moved with the times.[13]

The Cyclical Ups and Downs

Hampered by high interest rates coupled with soaring inflation, the homebuilding industry hit a slump in the early 1980s. By the end of 1982, Shea Homes was down to 35 employ-

ees and had started only 38 homes that year. It closed only 153, the fewest in any year since Shea Homes began in 1968.[14]

Following John Shea's short tenure as president of Shea Homes, Roy Humphreys was appointed president of Shea Homes in 1980, just in time to see the homebuilding business bottom out. Shea Homes liquidated its Nevada division that same year because the division was performing poorly, probably due to inadequate management. "So we were basically a two-division California company," Humphreys said.[15]

John Shea remembered one particularly trying time in the early 1980s. Shea Homes,

Right: Shea Homes' Reunion series homes near Denver, Colorado, are inspired by colonial, craftsman, Italianate, and Victorian farmhouse styles. Pictured is the Welcome Center.

Below: The Mission Viejo purchase included 22,000 acres in Colorado called Highlands Ranch. Residents of Highlands Ranch enjoy the approximately 60 miles of trails.

Sheas great homebuilders, but they're also good at land development. They're the kind of people you can make a handshake deal with and know they'll keep their word."[26]

"Negotiating with Morgan Stanley was really my first exposure to working with what I would call the Wall Street mentality, where you start a meeting at eight o'clock in the morning and you get it done by seven o'clock that night," said Les Thomas, president of Shea Homes Southern California. "Eventually we brought the portfolio to the Sheas [John, Edmund, and Peter] and walked them through it and talked about discount values and relative value of money over time and the opportunity that this was creating and the potential for future opportunities. They approved it, and we bought into a very large portfolio."[27]

Shea's joint venture with Morgan Stanley became even more important not long thereafter. A much larger deal was in the offing, the 1997 sale of the Mission Viejo Company by the Philip Morris Company. The sale was large enough that Shea wanted to partner with another company to put in a bid. Les Thomas contacted Morgan Stanley to see if it was interested, but Philip Morris had already hired Morgan Stanley to be its agent in the sale. After that, Shea and some of the other companies interested in the purchase planned to submit one bid among them and then split up the land. Philip Morris got wind of their plan, however, and said it would entertain only single-company bids in order to increase competition. Shea was forced to go it alone.[28]

The Mission Viejo Company acquisition required intense due diligence, and Shea didn't

Shea Homes received a number of awards and honors that recognized the superiority and creativity of its projects. By 1988, the year of its 20th anniversary, Shea Homes had built more than 9,000 homes, 2,000 apartment units, three mobile home parks, and two industrial parks. The Silver Creek Valley Country Club in San Jose, California (both pages), exemplified Shea Homes' knack for creating the ideal place to live.

have a lot of time. The assembled due diligence team proved worthy of the task, however. Because the asset holdings resided in Orange County, California, and Metro Denver, in Colorado, the team was made up of people from the J. F. Shea corporate office, Shea Homes Southern California, Shea Properties, and the newly formed Shea Homes Colorado.

"There was a very short timeline to get fully up to speed on the transaction and determine what we were willing to pay for the company," said Bert Selva, former division president of Shea Homes Colorado who succeeded Humphreys as president of Shea Homes. "Everyone worked well together, and there were many late nights—but it really paid off."[29]

John Morrissey, who acted as general counsel for Shea as a senior partner in a national law firm and later became Shea's senior vice president of legal and investments, described the atmosphere on the day Shea submitted its bid.

It was wild in the boardroom—kind of like a three-ring circus. While we were working on the bid, we were also conducting an auction-like bid process with the Ohio State Teachers over the ownership of Club Laguna. At the same time, we won a huge bid on construction. We were sitting around the table trying to decide what the bid price should be for Mission Viejo, and at the same time we'd have reports coming in from the Club Laguna auction. Then Peter walked in and said we'd won the heavy construction bid. At that point, I remember thinking, "Wow, this company has gotten really huge."[30]

Shea ended up winning the bid, despite the fact that another company had submitted a higher bid. "Philip Morris wanted no contingencies and a 30-day close, and we were able to give it to them," Shontere said.

Because Shea was a private company, it couldn't issue stock to raise capital and had to purchase with debt. Shea's bank group expanded the bank facility to accommodate the capital required. "We talked to Wells Fargo, which was our lead bank," Shontere said. "Wells

Shea Properties' beautiful Valentia apartments, in La Jolla, California, contain 318 units in six condominium-style buildings. Valentia offers a wide array of concierge services and conveniences designed for busy professionals.

CHAPTER EIGHT

SHEA PROPERTIES

1977–2004

*Shea Properties is a big part of our company. It's one of the ways we
stabilize our cash flow.*

—John F. Shea, President

IN 1977 SHEA CONTIN-
ued its strategy of diversification with the creation of a
property management company.
Originally called MALTA, Inc., the
name changed to Shea Business
Properties in 1985 and later
became simply Shea Properties.

Shea Properties eventually became one of
Shea's fastest-growing subsidiaries. Over the
years, it evolved into a multifaceted company
with responsibility for land acquisition, development, construction, and management of business parks, shopping centers, apartment communities, mobile home parks, and property
development. But the company had a slow start,
and not until the mid-1990s did it really come
into its own.

From Homebuilding to Property Management

Even before MALTA's creation, Shea had
been involved in buying and developing property,
mostly in California, through PBS Corporation
(later Shea Homes). It started in 1969 when
PBS finished building the apartment communities in Fountain Valley and Cerritos. That
same year, construction began on three mobile
home parks.

Like all true entrepreneurs,
the Sheas soon discovered that
some of their ideas just didn't
work out. "Our original intent was
to build the two apartment complexes and three mobile home
parks and then sell them," said
John Shea. "But the market was
a disaster, and we would have lost a lot of money,
so we held onto them. That's what put us into the
investment properties business."[1] Eventually,
two of the three mobile home parks were sold.

But for a while the Sheas decided to take
a turn themselves at selling mobile homes
within the parks. "We thought maybe we could
occupy our parks a little faster by doing this,
so we bought mobile homes and parked them
in our parks," said John Shea. "That was a
very unprofitable venture, and we finally quit
doing it. I don't know if there was no demand or
if we didn't know what we were doing. We were
kind of novices."[2]

The Sheas might have been novices, but
they knew they wanted to continue investing

Ocean Ranch II, in Laguna Niguel, California, is part
of Ocean Ranch Village, a master-planned community.

Both pages: The Waterford development in Dublin, California.

division, was a prime example of Shea's ability to compete in different sectors. Vistancia included plenty of housing, golf courses, and shopping centers, and whereas other companies would have to sell off pieces of the project to commercial developers, Shea Properties' diversity allowed it to take on part of the build-out.[20]

Vistancia also reflected Shea Properties' first move into Arizona, and the company planned to use its presence there as a launching pad to create Shea Properties Arizona.

In 2003 residential apartments made up about 70 percent of the portfolio in terms of market value, and commercial properties, including retail centers, industrial centers, and office buildings, made up most of the balance.[21]

Don Gause explained why the majority of Shea Properties' assets were in apartment complexes. "They're tremendous cash flow investments," he said. "They appreciate quite well. It's also one of the most consistent assets in commercial real estate investment."[22]

Gause considered 2003 to be a milestone year for Shea Properties, for it would be bringing four apartment properties to stabilization.

One of these was part of the Waterford development in Dublin, California, which included the Waterford Place apartment community and an adjacent shopping center called the Shops at Waterford.

"Waterford Place is getting a lot of press because it's unique," said Bob Burke, senior vice president for Shea Properties Northern California. "All the cities encourage mixed-use development because of the attractive retail sales tax component."[23]

Mixed-use refers to the unique relationship between the residential and retail space. A portion of the retail stores would be located on the

The luxury Victorian-style apartments of Sycamore Bay are located in California's Old Towne District of Newark.

Bill Gaboury joined Shea in 1984 as president of Shea Properties. He helped grow Shea Properties into a major real estate and asset management entity.

ground floor of the four-story apartment community, and as with City Lights, residents park on the same level as their apartments.

Recognizable Quality

Just like the other Shea companies, Shea Properties and its leaders earned their share of honors and accolades. In January 2001, Bill Gaboury was elected to the board of directors for the National Multi Housing Council (NMHC), which represents the nation's leading companies that participate in the apartment industry.

But perhaps the most prized tribute came in August 2002 when CEL & Associates, an independent survey firm in Los Angeles, honored Shea Properties with the 2002 National Multifamily Customer Service Award for Excellence.

"The award is given each year to the apartment management company which scores 'the highest' on a standardized nationwide survey of apartment residents," explained Steve Gilmore, senior vice president of the Apartment Communities Group. "Shea Properties scored best in our region and among the best in the nation."

Based on 2003 surveys, Shea was ranked third in the nation.

On the Rise

In addition to Steve Stambaugh, Lee Pacheco, Bob Burke, Don Gause, and Steve Gilmore, other key individuals with operating responsibilities included Jack Godard, senior vice president for commercial properties, and Gil Neilson, senior vice president for commercial property management.

Despite the poor economy in 2003, the future of Shea Properties looked bright. With interest rates near a record low, the housing market continued its healthy climb, and that promised to rub off on Shea Properties. More homes being built meant more retail and other services would be needed.

For the future, Shea Properties will find new properties to develop—whether through acquisition or joint venture—and continue leveraging the natural synergies between Shea Homes and Shea Properties. Gaboury also planned to focus on shopping centers and neighboring apartments because of their natural synergy, though the division would continue adding office buildings and industrial parks.

Gaboury envisioned Shea Properties continuing to increase its contribution to the parent company. "Shea Properties is a wonderful vehicle for Shea," he said. "We still produce cash flow, much of it tax deferred, even when the economy is slow, and we'll continue to grow our portfolio. We're a tremendous asset to the J. F Shea Co., Inc."[24]

Shea has been involved in venture capital since the late 1960s. The halls of Shea's headquarters are lined with plaques from Shea's venture capital investments.

CHAPTER NINE

VENTURE CAPITALISTS

1968–2004

The semiconductor and biotech revolution were the new Industrial Revolution as far as Shea was concerned.

—Edmund Shea, Executive Vice President

SHEA'S START AS A VENTURE capital company came in the late 1960s when Edmund Shea was in the San Francisco Bay area working on the BART projects. With his background in civil and electrical engineering, Edmund was able to detect a technological revolution percolating in nearby Silicon Valley and knew that Shea was in a prime position to take advantage. While many of the fledgling computer and biotech companies of that region would become well known, most of them were still laboring in anonymity.

Not many people realized it at the time, but the industrial world was shifting. The smokestack industries that Gil and Ed Shea had invested in after World War II, while still valuable, represented the past. The future belonged to the computer chip, semiconductor, software, and biotech companies, all of which would lead to a new kind of revolution.

"It became obvious that the world was changing rapidly and the 'smokestack' industries were being overshadowed by high-tech companies," Edmund Shea explained many years later. "In other words, the semiconductor and biotech revolution were the new Industrial Revolution as far as Shea was concerned."[1]

Getting Started

Edmund went to Bank of America to find out more about how he could get in on the ground floor of these up-and-coming technology companies. There he was introduced to George Quist, who led Bank of America Ventures. "George got me into a deal in San Diego with Bank of America," Edmund recalled. "Then George left Bank of America and joined up with Bill Hambrecht, who I found out was a good friend of my brother Peter."[2]

Hambrecht, also an investment banker, had become friends with Peter Shea while the two served together in the army. As a team, Hambrecht and Quist emphasized high-tech firms that, according to Peter Shea, were "still in the incubation stage" in Silicon Valley.

It was Quist and Hambrecht who guided the Sheas into venture capital. "We talked to them about coinvesting with them," Edmund recalled. "And they said, 'Well, why don't you invest in our investment banking firm, too?'"[3]

Compaq Computer is among the technology companies that Shea has invested in.

Edmund Shea, executive vice president of the J. F. Shea Co., Inc., spends much of his time handling Shea's venture capital investments.

Thus the Sheas joined Hambrecht & Quist (H&Q) as limited partners, owning the largest percentage of limited partnership shares in the firm. When H&Q went public, the Sheas became the third-largest stockholders. (Later, Edmund Shea joined H&Q's board of directors and served as a member until the firm was acquired by Chase Bank in the late 1990s.)

Although Shea continued to invest with H&Q, it also invested in venture capital start-ups independently and set up a Shea Ventures division, supervised by Edmund Shea, that was devoted to venture capital. The relationship with Hambrecht also continued. Edmund stayed on the H&Q board until a month before H&Q

was acquired by Chase Bank. Hambrecht then started another investment banking company called W. R. Hambrecht & Co. on February 1, 1998. Edmund and other Shea family members showed their confidence in Hambrecht by investing in his new company.

The Shea Style of Investing

It was 1968 when the J. F. Shea Co., Inc., began investing much of its heavy-construction income in start-up companies, with John, Peter, and Edmund Shea matching the company's investment dollar for dollar.

"The investing was very passive until about 1980," Edmund said. "Then I started spending about 75 percent of my time on the venture capital side and none on the construction side."[4]

Mostly the Sheas liked to get in on the first and second rounds of investing and avoided buying into public companies. Also, they were inclined to recycle the money or take it off the table two to three years after the company went public. The Sheas also tended to be silent investors, although Edmund Shea had joined some of the companies' boards. In his most active venture capital years, Edmund considered about 25 investments a year, most of which he became acquainted with after a fellow venture capital investor had prescreened them, although even Edmund acknowledged that "a lot of these deals were serendipity."[5]

Often Edmund decided to make investments based on the quality of the people involved. That's how he chose to invest in Activision, the home video game company. Activision started off successfully enough but declared bankruptcy after a few years. Meanwhile, an entrepreneur named Bobby Kotick had been looking to invest in a company that had licenses with some of the big home video game companies, including Sega and Nintendo, so he bought Activision out of bankruptcy. Now Kotick needed some other investors to help return the company to profitability. He explained his business plan to Edmund while they were sitting on the beach in Thailand. Edmund was taken with Kotick's "engaging personality," as well as the business plan. He also liked Kotick's business partner, Brian Kelly. Edmund ended up investing $5 million in Activision. "Bobby and Brian were a terrific management team," Edmund said. "They really managed Activision well."[6]

Edmund described why he enjoyed delving into venture capital. "It's like going to school," he said. "It's so intellectually challenging. You're looking at cutting-edge sciences years ahead of when they'll come to market. I really got hooked on the technologies."[7]

Lucrative Choices

By the turn of the century, Shea and the Shea family had made direct investments in more than 250 companies. These investments have included such successful companies as Adobe,

Altera Corporation, Apple Computer, Brocade, Compaq Computer, Massachusetts Computer, Linear Technology, and Lam Research in the computer and semiconductor industry; Genentech, Myriad Genetics, Xoma, Affymax, and ADAC Labs in the biotech and medical industry; and America West Airlines, AES Corporation, and Peet's Coffee & Tea in the industrial and commercial area, to name but a few.

Edmund named some of the most profitable investments Shea had made over the years: Angelo Gordon, Affymax, Altera, Dallas Semiconductor, Lam Research, and Genentech.

Shea's single most profitable investment was with AES Corporation, an independent energy company based in Arlington, Virginia. When Edmund read AES's business plan, he realized he knew the chairman and founder, Roger Sant, from the venture capital world. Sant's father had run a large homebuilding business in Southern California. Moreover, AES's business plan "was written like a real estate project," Edmund said.[8]

AES's great success didn't come right away.[9] Shea made its first investment in AES in the early 1980s, but not until 1996, when utilities were deregulated, did the company really take off. Deregulation allowed non-utility companies to own power generators, and AES built numerous plants in third-world countries.

Shea invested in Adobe when it was a start-up company and made a tidy profit but was unable to make a second round of investment.

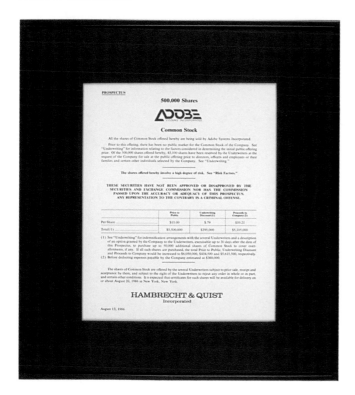

Regrets and Disappointments

There is no denying the extraordinary success of Shea's venture capital endeavors, but Edmund recalled some missed opportunities as well.

We put a relatively small amount of money into Adobe at first because it was a start-up company, and we wanted to see how it proceeded. As we followed it and tracked it, it really looked like a great visionary product and company opportunity. We were prepared to put a significant amount of money into the next round, but then Apple Computer swooped in and made a big corporate investment. As a result, we were unable to make a second round

of investment. We did make quite a profit on our initial round, but not being able to do the second round was a big lost opportunity.[10]

Not all of the Sheas' investments were in technology companies, and not all of them were successful. "I got hooked into the airlines," Edmund recalled. "First, America West Airlines, then Jet America. Jet America then got into a [market share] war with American Airlines out of Long Beach, and we eventually sold all the equipment to Delta. We also invested in Air South and Vanguard Airlines, both disasters. Air South failed pretty quickly, but Vanguard limped along for a while before it failed."[11]

Shea's investment in Osborne Computer, though unsuccessful, helped set a precedent for professional liability claims, especially in California. In 1982 Shea, along with numerous others, invested in Osborne Computer to help it ramp up its revenue before its attempt to go

Shea's venture capital investments cover a wide range of companies, including those in computer and semiconductor industries, biotech and medical industries, and industrial and commercial industries.

public. This type of "bridge lending" was especially popular in the 1980s and was a high-risk transaction that promised a high rate of return if successful.

Shea's decision to invest in the start-up portable computer company was based in part on an audit opinion by Arthur Young & Company. As it turned out, Osborne Computer was having substantial problems with its internal accounting controls, production, and marketing and went bankrupt before its public stock offering was completed.

The bridge lenders, including Shea as the lead investor, filed a lawsuit against Arthur Young, asserting the audit was negligent and contained errors. In 1986, after a 13-week trial, a jury ruled that Arthur Young was liable for professional negligence (but not intentional fraud) and awarded about $4.3 million to the investors. The appellate court affirmed the verdict. In effect, the ruling expanded an auditor's liability for negligence to anyone who used an audit report, regardless of whether the user was the auditor's client.[12]

In 1992, in *Bily v. Arthur Young & Company,* the California Supreme Court disagreed with the lower California court's decision, saying that "an auditor is a watchdog, not a bloodhound." The court ruled that only clients of the auditor could sue the auditor for negligence in audit reporting and restricted the auditor's liability to those cases where the auditor tried to influence the client with misrepresentations in the audit report.[13]

The court's decision set a standard for third-party liability in California, and as one reporter noted shortly after the ruling, "The California Supreme Court's opinion is likely to influence courts around the country."[14]

A Strong Base

In the late 1990s, Shea's venture capital investments accounted for a significant percent of the parent company's net worth—43 percent by year-end 2000—which was remarkable given that the company had not made any new venture capital investments and had been liquidating its positions in venture capital since 1983. In 1983 the company elected to retain its cash to support its capital-intensive operating businesses, especially Shea Homes and Shea Properties. John, Edmund, and Peter, who had previously split the venture investments with the company, continued to invest in venture capital with their own assets.

The company's portfolio took a huge dip in 2000 and 2001, along with the rest of the market. The company had been borrowing against the value of its marketable securities (i.e., borrowing "on margin") to supplement borrowings under its bank line of credit. When the stocks declined in value, the company's ability to borrow on margin was virtually eliminated. In September 2001, when the company had limited excess capacity under its bank line, the company sold a large block of stock in AES, the company's largest holding at that time, generating over $100 million in much need liquidity. On the same day the company executed this sale, AES issued a press release after the market closed that caused AES' stock price to decline by 50 percent on the following day. The timing of Shea's sale was fortunate: Had the company waited one day, it would never have realized the cash it needed because it would have been almost impossible to make a large block trade of AES stock at any price.

Even after Edmund Shea liquidated much of the company's venture capital investments, in 2003 it still had active investments in several companies, although the value of these investments as a percentage of Shea's net worth had declined.[15]

Shea Homes and Shea Properties benefited from Shea's venture capital investments. The increase in the value of the venture capital investments allowed Shea to compete with public homebuilders, who could sell stock to raise cash to buy sizeable pieces of land. Without the venture capital investments, it would have been more difficult for Shea to buy the Mission Viejo Company, the $473 million transaction that gave Shea Homes and Shea Properties key assets in California and Colorado.

Shea's venture capital endeavors were directly related to the company's growth, but they also manifested themselves in other ways. As one writer put it, although the privately held J. F. Shea Co., Inc., remained "a closely held private company with a zealously guarded low profile," proof of Shea's success in venture capital could be found on the walls of the J. F. Shea Co., Inc.'s office, which were "lined with framed evidence of the Shea-sponsored companies."[16]

This shot of a 32-foot-four-inch Robbins tunnel boring machine highlights the machine's gigantic proportions.

CHAPTER TEN

HEAVY CONSTRUCTION

1971–2004

We look at ourselves as being one of the leading American tunneling contractors. We've been in this business for a long time.

—Peter O. Shea,
President and CEO of J. F. Shea Construction

THE 1970S BROUGHT DRAmatic changes to the technology of the tunnel industry. Until then, hard-rock miners employed roughly the same methods—air drills and dynamite—that were used to build the transcontinental railroad in the 1860s. Soft-ground miners generally worked the same way they had when tunnels were driven under the Hudson River in the early years of the century. Although these tried-and-true methods were still used when conditions allowed for nothing else, the introduction of the gigantic tunnel boring machines (TBMs), nicknamed "moles," and earth pressure balance machines (EPBMs) changed everything.

"During my career, mining techniques have gone through an industrial revolution," observed Charles H. "Buck" Atherton, a Shea executive vice president and one of the world's leading tunnel experts.[1]

Atherton, whose construction career goes back to the mid-1950s, is one of the most honored men in the business. In 1991 he received the prestigious Golden Beaver Award for supervision. Six years later, he was given the Moles' Outstanding Achievement in Construction Award. These awards are the heavy construction industry's two highest honors, and Atherton was the only recipient of both who was not a company owner, CEO, or president.[2]

In his 1997 Moles' Annual Banquet acceptance speech, Atherton, who started working for the Sheas in 1967 as a project manager in San Francisco for the Bay Area Rapid Transit (BART) system, recalled some of the changes that revolutionized his business, many of which came to the forefront in the 1970s.

The typical rock tunnel job was mined using the drill-and-shoot method, with loaders used to load the tunnel muck onto rail cars that transported the material to a shaft or a portal. If it was a shaft project, the muck cars would be lifted off one at a time and hoisted to the surface.

Today we use tunnel boring machines (TBMs) to mine the rock, and we are increasingly using conveyor belts to transport rock out of the tunnel. If we have to take the rock up a shaft, we now use vertical belts.

Having been raised in heavy construction, Peter Shea always looked at home in a hard hat.

With these new techniques, we have driven in excess of 400 feet in 24 hours. Using the drill-and-shoot method, 50 or 60 feet would have been a good day.

Mining soft ground has also gone through radical changes. Today we use rotating cutter heads in shields or big diggers in shields that will give us up to 300 feet per day, compared to hand mining of 30 to 40 feet per day.

Not only do these advancements in mining techniques give us greater production, but they are much safer.[3]

Atherton recalled how things have changed in other ways. For example, when he began working for the Sheas, the company, for all practical purposes, had no home office. "John, Ed, and Peter were all project managers on tunnel jobs working out of trailers," he said. "This hands-on experience is still the Shea way."[4]

Jerry Toll, executive vice president for the Omaha-based construction firm of Peter Kiewit Sons', Inc.,—which "borrowed" Atherton from the Sheas in the early 1990s to help with a particularly troubled tunnel assignment in Denmark—offered another perspective on the changes in the tunneling business:

Forty years ago, when one piece of equipment went down, it was replaced with another piece of equipment. Today when one piece of equipment goes down, a hundred-thousand-dollar-a-day crew stands by while we figure out what to do.

The Sheas . . . are among the very few worldwide in the business who understand this equipment, who know how to make it work, who appreciate the earth and its ever-unfolding mysteries, and who can successfully match mining and materials. . . . While the equipment is different, the earth is still the same. It has not lost its ability to go instantaneously from friendly to mean, from hard to soft, to fracture, to run, to make water, to squeeze, to collapse, to chimney or to sink. . . . While there are only a few good miners, there are even fewer who understand the business of tunnel construction. In addition

to knowing how to mine, the businessman must recognize and understand the geology of working underground. He must be financially strong enough to underwrite the job start-up and survive job changes. He must be smart enough to solve the inevitable and occasionally catastrophic problems that arise in tunnel construction and be lawyer enough to resolve the disputes such problems entail. There are very few companies in North America who have these qualities and with whom Kiewit is willing to joint venture, and the Sheas stand high among them.[5]

The Washington Subway System

The Sheas used the new tunneling techniques and equipment on a major project for the first time when they began a series of subway tunnels, shafts, and stations for the Washington Metropolitan Area Transit Authority (WMATA) in 1971. Because it would serve the nation's capital, the project became known as "America's Subway."

WMATA was created in 1967 to build a rapid-rail system that connects the District of Columbia with suburban Virginia and Maryland. According to Jim Marquardt, project manager of WMATA's Greenbelt Route Subway Tunnel, in Hyattsville, Maryland, Shea was the first major contractor on the Washington subway system and ended up building more of the subway system than any other contractor.[6] Shea's first job for WMATA was to mine tunnels under the Potomac River.[7]

At the time, in the early 1970s, the construction work was organized by people and project. John Shea was running work in the West with Mike Shank as project manager. Edmund Shea began running work in the East with Buck

Over the years, Shea completed a number of jobs for the Washington Metropolitan Area Transit Authority (WMATA) to help build "America's Subway" in the Washington, D.C., area. Shea was the first major contractor on the subway system, winning the first contract in 1971, and built more than 14 miles of subway tunnels, shafts, and stations.

eight-mile, $54 million tunnel for the Bureau of Reclamation's Central Utah Project to provide irrigation to the state's Central Valley—the tunneling business began a decline that lasted into the late 1980s.

With prices driven below what they considered to be a reasonable profit level, the Sheas all but withdrew from heavy construction for a few years, a bold decision that would have been virtually impossible for a publicly held company, which must be sensitive to the interests of stockholders. By 1986 the Sheas' once-impressive $200 million heavy construction backlog was down to $20 million.

"We just kind of shrank ourselves down," Peter Shea said. "We did some very small tunnel jobs because much of the work was being bid at unprofitable rates."[24] This "shrinkage" would last for several years, but as a private company, Shea was not pressured to show earnings growth from one fiscal quarter to the next as public companies are.

The Sheas' decision proved to be the right one as they watched competitors rack up losses after chasing unrealistically priced projects. A few companies even went out of business.[25]

Infrastructure Work

Of course, not all the work disappeared. With tunnel work slow all over the country, Shea began bidding on infrastructure work instead. Active as ever, in 1978 Atherton opened an office in Chicago.

When the Environmental Protection Agency and the U.S. Congress mandated that cities clean up sewer and rainwater released into the Great Lakes and various rivers throughout the country, Shea won a $100 million contract for the Combined Sewer Overflow (CSO) project in Chicago to help clean up Lake Michigan. Other Chicago-area projects included the Randolph Street Pedestrianway, a variety of tunnel repair work, and three toll plazas and pedestrian tunnels for the Illinois Tollway Authority.

The major Chicago tunnels "consisted of many shafts 170 to 300 feet deep with under-ground chambers, and 32-, 19-, and 15-foot tunnels driven with TBMs and then concrete lined," said Atherton.[26]

Shea also built seven miles of sewer tunnel in Rochester, New York, for Rochester's $90 million CSO project, which lasted from 1980 to 1985. A Robbins TBM had to be specially rebuilt for the job.

Heavy Construction Recovers

By the late 1980s, the heavy construction market had recovered, and Shea was positioned to bid successfully on a variety of new projects. For many of these, Shea provided "value engineering"—that is, it improved the economics of the original design. The savings reaped from value engineering were usually split 50-50 between the contractor and the owner of the project.[27]

Shea continued doing work for the Washington Metropolitan Area Transit Authority (WMATA). In early 1991 Shea finished the 9,640 feet of soft-ground Greenbelt Route Subway tunnels in Hyattsville, Maryland, after having made a value-engineering change for the tunnel excavation. Shea also earned a bonus for running a safe job.[28] In 1993 Shea began the Glenmont Route tunnels, a $50 million job from WMATA that included more than 6,000 feet of twin tunnels, a vent shaft structure, and a traction power substation. Jim Marquardt was project manager, and Peter Shea, Jr., who graduated with an engineering degree from UC Berkeley in 1989, was project engineer.[29] In 1995 WMATA recognized Shea crews for working on the Glenmont Route tunnels for 25,000 hours without a lost-time incident (LTI). Of the four Metrorail tunnel projects then in progress, Shea had the best safety record.[30]

Opposite: Holing through on the second Greenbelt Route Subway Tunnel in Hyattsville, Maryland, one of several projects Shea did for WMATA. Shea made a value-engineering change for the tunnel excavation and earned a bonus for running a safe job.

Those in the Shea family who work at the company gather for a rare group photo in 2003. Front row, from left: Charlie Shea, Jim Shea, Mike Shea, Peter Shea, Jr., Peter Shea, Sr., John F. Shea, Alison Shea Knoll, Edmund Shea, John Morrissey, and Ed Shea III. Back row, from left: John F. Shea, Jr., Charlie O'Melveny, Gil Shea, Michael O'Melveny, Dan O'Melveny, Matt Shea, Chris Burget, and Joe Flanagan.

CHAPTER ELEVEN

A STRONG FOUNDATION

Here is a company that's going from the third to the fourth generation, and it's only becoming more successful. The J. F. Shea Co., Inc., keeps building on its success with each new generation because the Sheas have created an enterprise where people can prosper and contribute to that success.

—Jim Shontere, CFO

ALTHOUGH THE PREVIOUS decades were sometimes difficult for the J. F. Shea Co., Inc., in 2003 the company was more diverse and perhaps more widely respected than at any time in its history. On the 2003 *Forbes* magazine list of "The Largest Private Companies in America," J. F. Shea Co., Inc., ranked number 101 for the year ending 2002.

John, Edmund, and Peter Shea were among the construction industry's finest businessmen and most respected managers. For starters, they tended to be fiscally conservative but were still willing to take risks. In addition, no surety or lender had ever lost a penny on the Sheas, and they were remarkably consistent with the high ethical values handed down from the previous generation. They also offered independence to their managers, with top performance expected in return. And finally, the Sheas were approachable and cared about the people who worked for them.

The Men at the Top

Chief Financial Officer Jim Shontere, who joined the company in 1987, quickly learned that John, Edmund, and Peter Shea appreciated and respected each other, and that regard was reflected in their management style.

Shontere said he "learned early on that if you went to John and asked him a question about construction, he'd say, 'You need to talk to Peter because that's Peter's area.' When I brought up J. F. Shea Redding or investments, he'd say, 'You need to talk to Edmund because that's his area.' They really respect the autonomy and the authority of each other in their respective areas."[1]

Shontere also admired what he called "the family aspect" of the company. "The Sheas are very protective of their time," he said. "They're very focused when they're here. Very seldom do we engage in idle chitchat. They go home at five or six o'clock at night to their families, and that's the example they set for the rest of us."[2]

Sometimes it was the small things—the odd moments and little gestures, even if unintended—that people remembered and valued. "Peter Shea was always interested in going down into the tunnels and seeing just exactly what

Shea has one of the best safety records in the industry. The company's safety program starts at the top and involves all of Shea's employees and TradePartners®.

they're on the same level. At some companies, it takes you a month to get a stapler. At Shea, the attitude is 'What do you need?'"[16]

According to Roy Humphreys, Shea's culture is built on the foundation of respect for the customer and fellow employees. "Clearly our people view the company as theirs," he said. "That makes us more competitive in many arenas. . . . [When] everyone is working toward the same goals, everyone benefits from the company's success. It's an organization driven [to achieve] excellence."[17]

To ensure quality, Shea chose contractors based on the quality of their construction, safety records, and other criteria, rather than merely going with the lowest bidders. The com-

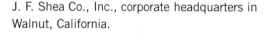

J. F. Shea Co., Inc., corporate headquarters in Walnut, California.

pany referred to these trade contractors as TradePartners®, treating them as long-term team members rather than just suppliers, subcontractors, or vendors. Shea even invited them to participate in employee training classes and surveyed them about their practices and their employees' performance.

"We were looking for a commitment, and we would choose our TradePartners® based on their concern about quality, safety, and the things that are important to us," said Jim Shontere. "All the financial companies we deal with are our business partners, too."[18]

"TradePartnering produces results," said Robb Pigg. "We've turned TradePartnering into a business principle: long-term working relationships based upon a common set of values is far better than revolving-door relationships with trade contractors."[19]

In the mid- to late 1990s, Shea also began to embrace Stephen Covey's philosophy, set forth in his enormously popular book *The 7 Habits of Highly Effective People.* Covey says true success encompasses a balance of personal and professional effectiveness, very much in concert with the Shea culture. Shea continues to provide its employees the opportunity to participate in this training.

Caring Since 1881

Perhaps the core philosophy of Shea is best summarized by the company's global branding campaign, which was launched in 2000. The phrase "Caring Since 1881" captured the themes that emerged after exhaustive research and hundreds of interviews with Shea employees.

Bill Pisetsky, vice president for sales and marketing of Shea Homes Southern California, led the two-year effort to develop a Shea brand to express what made the company unique. "Shea's level of caring is what sets us apart from our competitors," declared Pisetsky.[20]

"People tend to want to give their all here," said Alison Shea Knoll, daughter of President John Shea and director of marketing for Shea Homes Southern California. "We're a customer-

focused company, and people are proud to work here because they're hearing the positive comments made about Shea out in the field."[21]

John Shea's son Jim agreed. "We expect a lot out of our employees," he said, "but in return they expect a lot out of us. We have a very strong tradition of maintaining high business ethics, and that runs across the board: our customers, our vendors, and, of course, our employees."[22]

Or, as Bruce Varker, CFO of Shea Homes said, "The 'Caring Since 1881' slogan reflects the tradition, it reflects the trust, and it reflects the continuity and consistency of the company since its founding. We care for our customers, our TradePartners®, and our employees."[23]

The Fourth Generation

Especially during the late 1990s, the next generation of Sheas began taking increasingly active roles in the company.

In 1996 Peter Shea, Jr., who had joined the company full-time in 1990, became project manager for tunneling in a $63 million Clark-Shea joint venture for WMATA. He was project engineer on a hard-rock tunnel for the Washington, D.C., subway system and served as project manager on the Eastside Reservoir Project, which included construction of two tunnels and a spillway in Hemet, California, for the Metropolitan Water District (MWD) of Southern California. The Eastside Reservoir Project was part of an overall plan to create a 4,500-acre reservoir to virtually double Southern California's water storage capacity. Shea's portion of the job was a $32.5 million contract.

In heavy construction, Peter, Jr., worked for a number of Shea's tunnel experts,

Left: John F. Shea is president of the J. F. Shea Co., Inc. He has led the company since 1958.

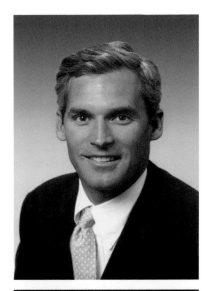

Top right: Peter Shea, Jr., grew up in the construction business. In 2002 he was promoted to chief operating officer of the J. F. Shea Co., Inc.

Center right: John Morrissey joined Shea in 2003 as senior vice president of legal and investments. For 10 years prior, he had been providing legal advice to Shea.

Below right: Jim Shontere joined Shea in 1987 as CFO. Thanks to his leadership, the J. F. Shea Co., Inc., has kept a conservative balance sheet and strong internal controls.

including Ed Marcus, Buck Atherton, and Norm Hutchins. "He caught on very quickly," Hutchins remembered. "And I think in those early jobs was when he learned to love tunnels."[24]

On his way to assuming a greater leadership role at the J. F. Shea, Co., Inc., Peter, Jr., spent more and more of his time at the corporate office. He also worked at Shea Homes and Shea Properties while still keeping up with heavy construction. "I knew I wanted to take a leadership role in the company

since I was pretty young," he said. "I felt I needed to learn the engineering side first, like John, Ed, and my dad did, and then it would be easier to learn the homebuilding and real estate industry, so that's what I did."[25]

Peter, Jr.'s plan paid off. On March 18, 2002, he was named chief operating officer of the J. F. Shea Co., Inc.

Meanwhile, other fourth-generation Sheas were moving up the company's ranks. Jim Shea, son of President John Shea, was project engineer on an $8 million tunnel in San Diego, part of the North City Tunnel Connector project. In 1999 Jim was named president of REED Manufacturing. In addition, Tim Shea, son of Executive Vice President Edmund Shea, served as project engineer on a $37 million drill-and-shoot twin tunnel job for the Arkansas Highway and Transportation Department.

In February 2003, John Morrissey, son-in-law of Edmund Shea, joined the next generation of up-and-coming Sheas when he became the company's senior vice president of legal and investments. Morrissey devoted most of his time to the company's and the Shea family's investment and venture capital activities. But he also provided legal advice to the company, as he had for the previous 10 years as a senior partner in Bingham McCutchen, a national law firm. For the near term, Morrissey planned to spend about half his time learning about and handling Shea's venture capital portfolio. The rest of his time would be split between providing legal service for the company and management of the overall enterprise.

As of 2003, 18 family members (including John, Edmund, and Peter) worked in the J. F. Shea Co., Inc. Peter Shea, Jr., Jim Shea, and John Morrissey were in top management positions. John (son of John Shea), Gil (nephew of John Shea), and Ed (son of Edmund Shea) headed up Shea Homes Charlotte. Other family members included Michael Shea (grandson of the elder Gilbert Shea), Alison Shea Knoll (daughter of John Shea), Matthew Shea (son of John Shea), Dan O'Melveny, Michael O'Melveny, and Charlie O'Melveny (all nephews of John

Shea), Joe Flanagan (son-in-law of John Shea), Charles A. Shea IV (great-grandson of Charlie Shea), and Chris Burget (great-grandson of Charlie Shea).

Emerging Opportunities and Challenges

The next generation of Sheas faced its own set of challenges, for as Shontere explained, it was impossible to replace the experience and tradition personified by John, Edmund, and Peter Shea. "But Shea has great management—people who have been with the company for years and who know it well," he said. "The Shea families and the people we deal with are confident that Shea's values and work ethics will stay consistent."[26]

The next generation faced another challenge: homebuilding and income properties made the company infinitely more complex than it had been for previous generations. "In the past, you basically wound down one construction company and started up a new construction company," Humphreys said a few months before his retirement in 2002. "Homebuilding offers a different challenge because it's a bigger monster. The key is to make sure that there's a transition that's visible so that the employees continue to feel empowered to run the business."[27]

Peter Shea, Jr., would like to see the heavy construction division grow to balance the real estate side of the business. "It would be beneficial to grow the heavy construction because the real estate business is very capital intensive, and heavy construction provides substantial cash for the growth of real estate," he explained. "Most of our heavy construction jobs are financed by the owner, which creates a wonderful balance between real estate and heavy construction."[28]

By the spring of 2003, it looked as if Peter, Jr., might be getting his wish, for Shea's heavy construction backlog was at its highest point ever. "That's sort of an anomaly," he said. "Usually heavy construction tends to be countercyclical to homebuilding."[29]

At the same time, Peter, Jr., wanted to continue growing Shea Homes, "first organically," he said. "Then we'll probably expand into new markets." He also wanted Shea Homes and Shea Properties to take better advantage of their obvious synergies. "We want to have more of an integrated real estate company, which will help us attain bigger projects because we'll be able to offer one-stop shopping."[30]

While he did not rule out future acquisitions—in fact, he believed there would be more—Peter, Jr., knew they demanded caution. "If there's an acquisition opportunity that goes back to our core philosophy, we probably will look at it a lot closer rather than trying to buy companies just for the sake of getting bigger," he said. "That's been the wonderful philosophy of my father and uncles, and it's worked."[31]

All of Shea's leaders agreed they wanted to keep the company private and family owned and managed. Though several of the company's operating businesses were run by nonfamily members, the Shea family—principally John, Edmund, and Peter—continued overseeing the businesses as a sort of resident board of directors. As the Shea family grew, the number of owners was growing larger, too, which meant communication would be crucial to the company's strength.

At the same time, all of Shea's leaders expected to grow the company while maintaining the traditions begun in 1881 with John Francis Shea. Since that time, the Shea name has been associated with quality and caring, and that legacy would continue as Shea's leadership made the gradual transition from John, Edmund, and Peter to the fourth generation of Sheas.

Edmund, Peter, and John Shea depart from a meeting at the headquarters building of J. F. Shea, Co., Inc., and Shea Homes. Behind them are (from left) Peter Shea, Jr., Charlie Shea, and John Morrissey.

COMMUNITY ACTIVITIES

THE J. F. SHEA companies are grateful for the success they've enjoyed over the years and have a strong desire to give back to the communities that have supported them in their growth. That's why the Sheas established the J. F. Shea Foundation and the Shea Homes Foundation, both of which contribute to charitable causes—including schools, cultural programs, and hospitals—within communities where the Shea companies operate. In addition, John, Edmund, and Peter Shea each set up his own philanthropic foundation.

Closest to the hearts of the Sheas has been a strong commitment to better education for disadvantaged youth in the inner cities. One recent example of that commitment was the foundation's $4.7 million donation to refurbish Verbum Dei High School in South Central Los Angeles. Shea Properties built the school's first regulation gymnasium and football field, as well as a library, cafeteria, additional classrooms, and an all-purpose center.

Another example of that commitment was the John

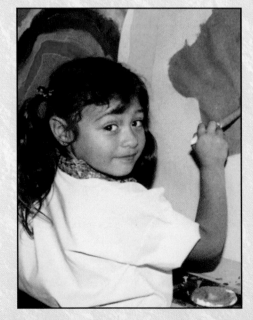

and Dorothy Shea Foundation's $7 million donation to refurbish Salesian High School in the East Los Angeles Community of Boyle Heights. Shea Properties assisted in supervising the construction of a 1,350-seat lighted football and soccer stadium, plus a three-level athletic building that has a basketball gymnasium, locker rooms, training center, and coaches' offices.

On behalf of the Shea foundations and the John and Dorothy Shea Foundation, in 2003 Shea Properties was managing the construction of two new gymnasiums, several new classrooms, and the renovation and retrofit of five inner-city schools in Los Angeles and Orange Counties.

Shea Properties and the Shea foundations also participated in constructing a new recreational facility for at-risk youth in Boyle

Heights. The Shea foundations and several other foundations, as well as the city of Los Angeles, made financial contributions to the $3 million project.

The Shea foundations have worked with public school systems in California, Arizona, and Colorado, making many contributions to prekindergarten programs for at-risk children as well as to programs for older students. On the parochial side, Shea made a $2.2 million donation toward refurbishing Bourgade Catholic High School in Phoenix, and Shea Homes Phoenix was the general contractor. It has also built kindergartens on more than 30 Catholic school sites, predominantly in low-income neighborhoods in Los Angeles County, and provided computer classrooms at a majority of these sites.[1]

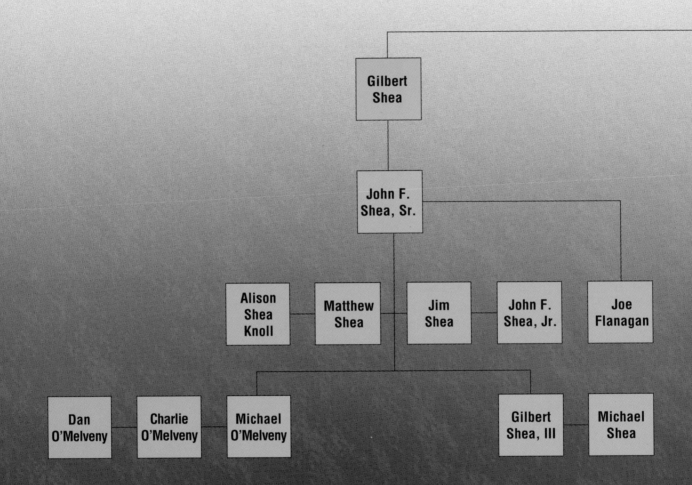

Gilbert
Shea

John F.
Shea, Sr.

Alison
Shea
Knoll

Matthew
Shea

Jim
Shea

John F.
Shea, Jr.

Joe
Flanagan

Dan
O'Melveny

Charlie
O'Melveny

Michael
O'Melveny

Gilbert
Shea, III

Michael
Shea

First Generation
JOHN FRANCIS SHEA (1855–1926), company founder

Second Generation
CHARLES A. SHEA (1883–1942), son of John Francis Shea
GILBERT SHEA (1896–1973), son of John Francis Shea
EDMUND H. SHEA (1898–1966), son of John Francis Shea

Third Generation
JOHN F. SHEA, SR. (born 1926), son of Gilbert Shea

EDMUND H. SHEA, JR. (born 1929), son of Edmund H. Shea
PETER O. SHEA, SR. (born 1935), son of Edmund H. Shea

Fourth Generation
MICHAEL SHEA (born 1971), grandson of Gilbert Shea
ALISON SHEA KNOLL (born 1969), daughter of
　　　John F. Shea, Sr.
MATTHEW SHEA (born 1974), son of John F. Shea, Sr.
JIM SHEA (born 1962), son of John F. Shea, Sr.

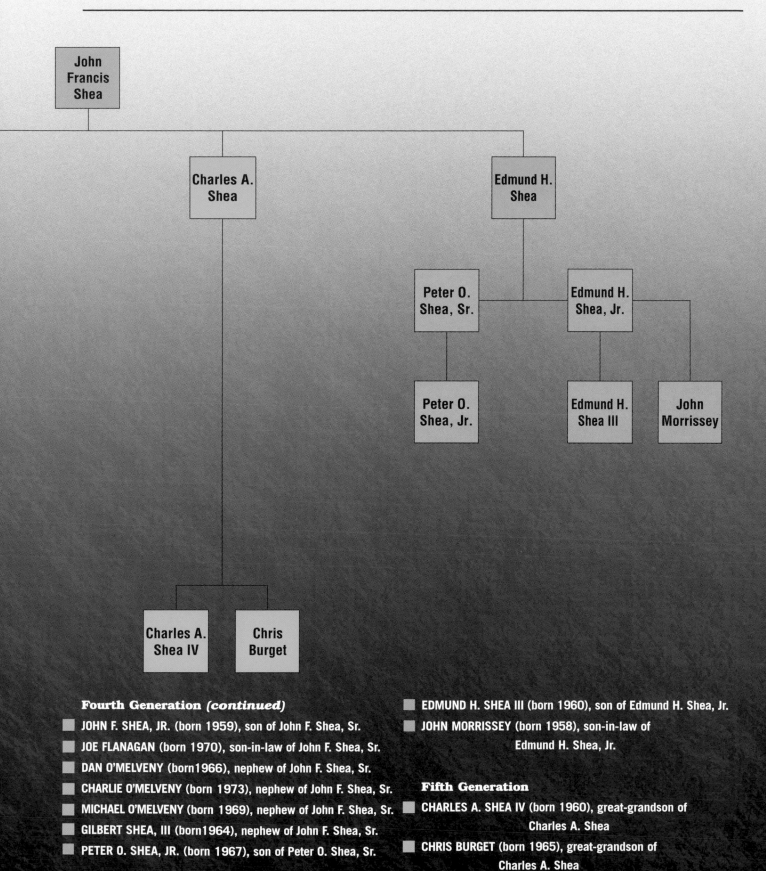

Fourth Generation *(continued)*

■ JOHN F. SHEA, JR. (born 1959), son of John F. Shea, Sr.

■ JOE FLANAGAN (born 1970), son-in-law of John F. Shea, Sr.

■ DAN O'MELVENY (born1966), nephew of John F. Shea, Sr.

■ CHARLIE O'MELVENY (born 1973), nephew of John F. Shea, Sr.

■ MICHAEL O'MELVENY (born 1969), nephew of John F. Shea, Sr.

■ GILBERT SHEA, III (born1964), nephew of John F. Shea, Sr.

■ PETER O. SHEA, JR. (born 1967), son of Peter O. Shea, Sr.

■ EDMUND H. SHEA III (born 1960), son of Edmund H. Shea, Jr.

■ JOHN MORRISSEY (born 1958), son-in-law of
Edmund H. Shea, Jr.

Fifth Generation

■ CHARLES A. SHEA IV (born 1960), great-grandson of
Charles A. Shea

■ CHRIS BURGET (born 1965), great-grandson of
Charles A. Shea

1881: John Francis Shea founds the J. F. Shea Plumbing Company, the predecessor of the J. F. Shea Co., Inc.

1920s: Shea develops a specialty in tunneling, and completes such important infrastructure projects as the Mokelumne Pipeline in California and the Owyhee Irrigation Project in eastern Oregon.

1930s and 1940s: Shea continues building history, taking part in such important public works projects as Parker Dam and Bonneville Dam. The company also helps build Liberty Ships for the British during World War II.

1915: The plumbing company is dissolved, and the J. F. Shea Company is formed, run mainly by three of John's sons, Charlie, Gil, and Ed.

1930s: As part of the Six Companies joint venture, Shea helps build Hoover Dam, the Golden Gate Bridge, and the San Francisco–Oakland Bay Bridge.

1958: The third generation of Sheas— John, Edmund, and Peter—form the J. F. Shea Co., Inc.

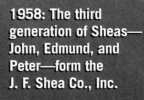

1960s onward: John, Edmund, and Peter continue the company's expertise in heavy construction, helping to build numerous public works projects, including the nation's interstate highway system, the Bay Area Rapid Transit system, the Washington, D.C., Subway system, the California Aqueduct, and the Chicago Deep Tunnel System.

Late 1960s: The Sheas began investing in venture capital, under the direction of Edmund Shea, Jr., in such lucrative companies as AES Corporation, Altera, and Genentech.

1997: Shea buys the Mission Viejo Company, adding thousands of acres of premium land to its homebuilding and property development assets. The following year, Shea buys UDC Homes.

1968: Shea forms PBS Corporation, the predecessor to Shea Homes. Over the years, Shea Homes grows from its California roots, with operations in Colorado, Arizona, North Carolina, and Washington.

1977: The company forms Shea Properties, which later experiences significant growth. It is responsible for land acquisition, development, construction, and management of commercial properties.

2004: The J. F. Shea Co., Inc., now well into the next century, is more diversified than at any time in its history as it continues to grow Shea Homes, Shea Properties, J. F. Shea Construction, Shea Financial Services, J. F. Shea Redding, and Partners Insurance Corporation.